DAVID'S

DECEPTION

SABRENA JAY

DEDICATION

I give honor to my Lord and Savior, Jesus Christ, who guides us along life's journey—through long roads and uncertain paths—until we emerge stronger, wiser versions of our former selves. It's through the abundance of his loving grace that I've been granted multiple chances to triumph at this journey called life.

TABLE OF CONTENTS

POEMS

Acknowledgements

I want to express my gratitude for my family, friends, and children. Your unconditional love has been my anchor through both sunny days and stormy nights. In moments when I felt depleted, you provided resources, helping hands, and unconditional love to revive me. I also want to give a special recognition to my husband and my girls, Laurie and Marla, your words of encouragement have meant more to me than you'll ever know. Thank you for being God's heartbeat here on earth.

It has taken me 17 years to share my journey, and it has indeed been an incredible one. I initially waited for a larger audience, hoping to expand my following as a speaker before sharing my story with the masses. One day, however, Jesus whispered in my ear, "Will you do it for the one? In this era of social media, many are focused on appealing to the masses, but regardless of the numbers, are you willing to share your testimony for the ONE person who needs to hear it?"

If you are reading this, then you are that ONE. I pray that my journey inspires you to discover the beauty of God's purpose in your own.

PREFACE

FAULTY FOUNDATIONS

Love can be a deadly sin. Many women sin every day behind the love of a man, the wrong man. I'll never understand how the devil can take something as pure as love and use it for evil. How can something that brings one person so much joy and happiness cause another such pain? And what is it about a man that can make a woman lose herself? Is it their looks, their charm, or just the fear of being without one?

I knew someone who gave her all to a relationship that provided nothing in return except heartache and pain. Yet, she clung to that unfruitful union until she died from AIDS—before him, no less. As she lay on her deathbed, I wonder if she realized that she was dying because she lacked the strength to let go of something that wasn't worth holding onto.

Had she mustered the willpower to move on, she could have embraced the life God intended for her to live—a life where authentic love abides. But when we constantly chase after people who are beyond our grasp, we hinder the flow of God from ushering in a love that remains for a lifetime.

So, why do we do it? Why do we settle for relationships built on faulty foundations, as unstable as quicksand? The answer lies in four words: Fear of Being Alone.

Loneliness is a power all its own, and the measures we take to avoid feeling its sting is astounding. At the expense of spending time alone with God and discovering who we truly are, we trade temporary discomfort for long-term hurt and pain. Failing to realize that any season of isolation is a gift - a time of refinement where God takes the time to introduce you to you - knowing the real tragedy of life is to live, die and never have the pleasure of making your own acquaintance.

However, as the saying goes, hindsight is 20/20, and wisdom is derived from experience. Having been someone who once traded temporary discomfort for long-term heartache and pain, this is my story of how God transformed my brokenness into a beautiful journey towards self-love, purpose, peace, and joy.

Chapter 1

Reflections

"It's my birthday, David. Are you really not spending any time with me today?" Those were the words I spoke to my boyfriend of six years as we drove back from taking two of our children to my aunt's house.

"I told you I have plans, and besides, you still have King with you," he said, trying to justify leaving me alone on my birthday.

"What am I supposed to do with him? I can't find anyone to watch him because you have him spoiled."

David dismissed my words as if my birthday was meaningless. "Look, I agreed to drop Katie and Kevin off, but that's all I have time for. Just be thankful that you have two fewer kids today."

A wave of depression surged through me—a feeling that had become all too familiar. "Well, here's my new cell phone number. If you finish early, can you call me, please?"

"Yeah, alright," he agreed, but his tone suggested otherwise.

Certain that this would be the last time I heard from him, I got out of the car with our 13-month-old son, slammed the door, and exclaimed, "This is going to be the worst birthday ever!"

He shook his head and drove away.

Lying on the bed of my overpriced Miami Lakes apartment, a fresh wave of despair washed over me. I looked around the room and pondered, 'How did I end up here? How did I end up with three kids at the age of twenty-two? It doesn't matter that two of them are twins; three kids at twenty-two is far too many.

How did I end up in this empty apartment on my birthday, jobless, penniless, and with only my toddler for company—whom, at the moment, I wish wasn't here?'

I sat up and surveyed the emptiness of a room that was designed to hold so much more: a 19-inch television sitting on a chair, a baby crib against the wall, and a mattress on the floor. That was pretty much all my room consisted of.

"I'm not supposed to be here!" I shouted. "I'm supposed to be in the Navy, traveling the world." That was my original plan after high school, but a mishap in basic training quickly derailed those plans. I was discharged after a few short weeks, and without a contingency plan, I came back home with only one thought in mind… David Hall.

Life lesson #1: Always have a plan B!

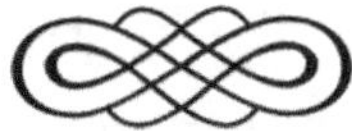

I'll never forget the day that man walked into my life. It was my senior year in high school, and I was a cashier at the local grocery store. One Friday afternoon, the store was particularly busy, and I longed to return home and climb into bed. Needless to say, I was providing less than superior service that day.

I didn't notice when he walked in, but when I looked up, there he stood: tall, light-skinned, and undeniably handsome. My stomach fluttered as I assisted my customer, trying to avoid his sexy stare. This continued for a couple of minutes before finally, my mystery man spoke. "Excuse me, my homeboy thinks you're cute."

I looked at his homeboy standing next to him — unattractive and overweight - rolled my eyes, and returned my attention back to my customer. He chuckled and walked away, leaving me feeling foolish for assuming that someone like him would be even remotely interested in someone like me (no doubt, I struggled in the self-esteem department).

Later that evening, the cashier from the service counter, Peggy, approached. "Hey, did you notice the light-skinned guy with dreads who was in my line earlier?"

"Yeah, I saw him," I replied, reliving the disappointment.

She reached into her pocket and took out a piece of paper. "He asked me to give this to you. It's his number."

I took the paper and without hesitation threw it into the waste bin.

"Girl, I'll take the number if you don't want it. That brother was fine. You're crazy."

"That number belongs to his friend," I said with a sigh.

"No, he said it was 'his' number," she insisted.

"It's a setup, girl. I'll pass." I left the paper in the trash, where it could do my fragile self-esteem no further harm.

I pushed all thoughts of my mystery man out of my mind until the following Friday when I caught a glimpse of his lean frame walking through the parking lot. As if on cue, I started fixing my hair and straightening my clothes. The lady whose groceries I was scanning looked confused, but I didn't care. My attention was on something far more tantalizing than her jars of jam.

Our eyes locked the moment he graced the sliding doors. He glanced in my direction and then walked to the service counter. Mesmerized, I analyzed his body from head to toe—look at those arms and those lips; I bet he's a good kisser.

Interrupted by my customer's sigh, I shifted my attention away from Mr. Handsome and resumed scanning her groceries... and scanned them I did. In fact, I nearly broke her jars.

When I returned my attention to the service counter, he was gone. My eyes roamed the store, searching for any sign of him. I looked out the window just in time to see his arm hanging out the window of a brown Chevrolet that was driving off.

'He drives a Chevy too? He is my dream come true!' Instantly, the disdain I felt from our previous interaction faded, replaced by an even stronger desire to make his acquaintance.

Third Time's a Charm

I wasn't entirely certain, but it seemed our store had become his preferred place to cash his paycheck. With that in mind, I arrived early on Friday and requested to work the service counter, unaware of the full magnitude of my request.

With everyone either buying cigarettes, cashing checks, or playing the lotto, I worked nonstop the entire afternoon. When I finally had a moment to look up, I caught sight of his tall frame standing at the end of my line. My hands instantly trembled in anticipation of our impending transaction.

After what felt like an hour, he reached the front of the line, this time accompanied by another guy who was equally as handsome. I assisted his friend, and then with the sweetest voice I could muster, turned to my mystery man and asked, "How can I help you today?"

"Hey, you didn't give me the change."

Confused by his remark, I stood there with a blank expression until I heard the voice again, "Where's my change?"

Suddenly, I realized the words weren't coming from Mr. Wonderful, but from the friend I had just assisted.

"Excuse me?" I responded. "I gave you the correct change."

"No, you gave me the paper bills, but not the coins."

"Can you check your pockets, please?" I said, rushing him along.

"That won't help. I already had change in my pocket."

I glanced at his receipt...17 cents? Was he really holding up my line over 17 cents?

I turned to my mystery man, who was now standing within arm's reach and stated, "I gave him his change, right?"

He dropped his head and smiled.

"It's no big deal," said the friend, "but I know you didn't give it to me."

Growing increasingly impatient, I reached into my pocket and pulled out a coin. "Here's a quarter; keep the change."

"That's alright, Love. You keep it." He smirked and walked away.

Finally, the magical moment I anticipated all afternoon had arrived… or so I thought.

Instead of the fireworks I had imagined, our exchange was quite uneventful. He quietly stood there while I cashed his paycheck, and once I provided him with the 'correct' change, he turned and walked away.

"Are you kidding me?" I muttered under my breath. 'I worked this busy service counter all afternoon just for the chance to speak with him, and he just walks away?' That sealed it. For the remainder of my shift, I had an attitude with every single customer that came my way.

At the end of the night, I was tallying up my drawer in the back office when Peggy strolled in and gave my ego a much-needed boost. "Okay, let's try this again. His name is David Hall, and this is his number. He said he's been checking you out for a while and likes what he sees. If you're interested, give him a call."

I looked at the paper in her hand, feeling both relief and reluctance.

"Honey, you better take it this time because I was tempted to keep it for myself."

I grabbed the paper and smiled, thinking she didn't have a chance, being that she looked more like Piggy than Peggy.

On the bus ride home, I sat with my mystery man's number in hand, daydreaming about the possibilities. Could he actually become my boyfriend? With limited dating experience, I started to feel unworthy of the one thing my heart truly desired – a relationship.

As my insecurities grew, I contemplated tossing his number once more. Nonetheless, I took a deep breath and decided to give it a shot. 'And if it doesn't work out, so what?' I was mentally prepared to handle the inevitable.

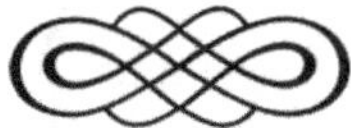

The following day, I woke up eager to speak with Mr. Hall. I finally got the opportunity later in the day, after my mom had left.

I called, and the sound of his deep voice saying "hello," gave me goosebumps.

Our conversation got off to a smooth start, and after a series of questions, I learned that he was 21 (four years my senior), had a two-year-old daughter, and lived with his grandma, uncle, and younger brother. I also discovered that he worked at the same warehouse as my dad and my cousin Faye.

After going over the formalities, we shared a few laughs about the game of 'eye hockey' we had been playing the past two weeks. The call concluded with pleasantries, and we agreed to talk again.

I cautioned myself not to get my head in the clouds. After the whirlwind I experienced with my last attempt at love, I wanted to avoid revisiting that pain at all costs.

A brief romance I had with the pastor's son came to an abrupt end when, in front of God and the congregation, I found out he was marrying another girl and joining the military. Not only was I devastated, but because his wedding was part of our Sunday service, I had the displeasure of being in attendance.

David seemed nice enough, but after finally unmasking my mystery man, I couldn't shake the feeling that I was headed towards an even greater level of heartache and pain.

This brings me to life lesson #2:
Trust your instincts.

CHAPTER 2

BROKEN FROM THE START

Captivated by my new crush, I slipped in phone calls whenever I could. Despite my efforts to remain guarded, David had a knack for putting me at ease.

One evening after finishing my shift, I stepped outside to find him and his Chevy waiting. I couldn't help but feel like a princess, especially when I noticed Peggy and another cashier spectating.

When I got into the car, he introduced me to his younger brother who was in the back seat. "Patrick, meet Sabrena. I'd call her my new lady, but we barely talk on the phone or see each other, so I'm not sure what we're doing."

I playfully dismissed his comment, but internally, panic set in. I knew he would eventually notice my lack of availability, but what options did I have?

At the age of 17, a senior in high school, my mom and step-dad were so strict that I wasn't even allowed to talk to boys on the phone. Having a beeper was prohibited (though I secretly carried one), and the very notion of having a boyfriend was out of the question. In fact, I was forced to quit a job after one of the guys I'd been flirting with obtained my phone number from the employee contact sheet and called the house.

"I'm sorry, but Sabrena isn't allowed to speak to boys on the phone," was the response that sent shivers down my spine.

Soon after, my mom took issue with my late hours and insisted that I resign.

Haunted by that experience, I was determined not to repeat the same mistake with David. I went to great lengths to avoid any potential issues, even blocking his number on the house phone in case he attempted to contact me.

To make matters worse, my free time was limited. My weekly schedule consisted of school, work, and home— unlike my sophomore year when I was in the school band.

If I wanted to hang out with friends after school or on the weekend, I'd use band practice as my 'get out of jail free card,' but what options did I have now?

Suddenly, I had an epiphany! To make this relationship work, I would have to resort to the same measures any teenager with overly strict parents would take: lying and sneaking.

From that moment on, skipping school and fabricating stories about my whereabouts became a regular part of my routine.

I eventually had to come clean with David about my situation, especially after he discovered his number was blocked. Of course, he wasn't fond of having to sneak around at his age, but I assured him that my plan would allow us to spend more time together.

Reluctantly, he agreed, and I was thrilled to officially be in a relationship with the man of my dreams. Well, you know what they say: Be careful what you wish for because you just might get it.

David was about to introduce me to another aspect of this equation that was more than I had bargained for.

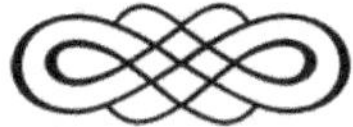

One day, I slipped out of school during lunch and hopped on the bus to his house. We were in the yard playing around when my knuckles brushed against his chin. "Wow, you nearly broke my jaw," he said, massaging his face.

"Whatever," I laughed. "I barely touched you."

"Naw, you punched me hard. So, how are you going to make it feel better?" he asked with a devious grin.

'Oh, he wants a kiss?' Well, it took him long enough. It had been weeks since we met, yet still hadn't kissed.

I gently cupped his face with my hands, "Let me see, you big baby."

He smiled, and for the first time I saw his teeth. Let's just say they didn't quite harmonize with the rest of his dreamy features. The front teeth overlapped, and the bottom row had teeth fighting for space. Upon closer inspection, I noticed a black speck in the middle of his front teeth. Was it food, a cavity, mystery meat?

There I stood, cradling his face in my hands, wondering what to do next. Before I had a chance to decide, he leaned forward and placed his lips over mine.

I can't recall whether it was a good kiss or not. However, what remains vivid is the sinking feeling that washed over me when he smiled, and the black substance between his teeth was gone. 'Oh, my goodness, please don't tell me that mystery meat is in my mouth!'

In the midst of my inner panic, a car pulled up and a very attractive female got out. David glanced in her direction and said he would be right back. At that moment, his teeth were the least of my concerns. I needed to know: who was this chick coming to see my man?

After a brief conversation, they walked over and David introduced her, "This is Ebony; she's a very good friend I've known since high school."

I greeted her, and in return, she gave me the proverbial up-and-down scan that women often give each other.

I suddenly felt very self-conscious.

"What do you have in here to drink?" she asked, walking past us into the house. David trailed behind her, and I stood there thinking, 'What just happened here?'

Upon entering the house, I found them in the kitchen talking. "Can you ride with me to take care of something?" she asked, taking a sip of water.

"No problem, but we have to drop Sabrena off first." They both looked at me, and I managed an awkward smile.

The ride home was just as uncomfortable. I sat in the backseat while David rode in the front. Engrossed in conversation, they chatted with each other as I silently stared out the window. Suddenly, thoughts of inadequacy, which always seemed to be lurking in the back of my mind, rose to the surface and I was ready for our little joy ride to end.

When we arrived in my neighborhood, I couldn't possibly get out at the corner, as per my usual routine, and let on that I was sneaking around. Determined to maintain some form of dignity, I directed her straight to my house and prayed for the best.

You can imagine my relief when she pulled into our empty driveway. "I'll see you later," I said softly as I exited the car.

David leaned out of the window, and I hoped he wasn't expecting another kiss. "I'll pick you up from work tomorrow, okay?" He smiled. I simply nodded in agreement.

I walked away feeling very small. I never understood why I tended to shrink in comparison to other girls. It was a defense mechanism tracing back as far as I can remember. Boy likes me, I like boy; boy sees girl...I hook them up. They date happily ever after, and I tell myself it didn't matter.

Oh, but this time it mattered. I was risking the wrath of my mom just to be with him – the mystery man whom I didn't feel worthy of dating but somehow was. He mattered, and I would no longer try to convince myself that he didn't.

As I turned the key to unlock the front door, a burning question lingered in my mind: 'Were they really just friends? But why would she offer me a ride if they were dating?'

I pushed the thought aside, reminding myself that I was dealing with a man, not a high school boy. I needed to adjust my mindset if I wanted things to work out. After all, it was evident that he liked me. I just had to become the type of woman he was accustomed to dating.

From that day forward, those were the words I recited whenever I had the nagging feeling that something about David wasn't quite right.

BE STILL, MY HEART

I can feel it pounding
at the very thought of you,
trying to break through
wanting you
to have, to hold
this beating rhythm in my soul

Be still, my heart
constant pounding in my chest,
who can put this sound to rest?
knocking on the door to my soul
but that's a key no man can hold

Yet, I let you in
into my heart,
into my mind,
into the very depths of me

For the love of you, I did things
I thought I'd never do

But then you went and broke my heart,
and tore my world apart,
tore it into a thousand pieces,
and sent it flying to the wind,
leaving my soul to run for cover

But there was none to be found

So now I've taken back my heart,
and returned it to its protected place,
never to come out and love again.
Yet, I have to wonder:
Will this pounding ever end?

Be still, my heart

CHAPTER 3

THE DILEMMA

Three months later, David and I were still going strong. Since they worked together and she sympathized with my situation, my cousin Faye allowed me to stay at her house on the weekends to spend more time with him. After some time, my mom noticed a shift in my behavior and grew suspicious.

One particular Friday, I returned from school to an empty house and decided to seize the opportunity for some quality time with Mr. Hall. The plan was to spend the majority of the evening with him, and then go to Faye's house afterwards. With that in mind, I left my mom a note and called the man I had grown quite fond of to pick me up.

Around eight o'clock that evening, David and I found ourselves lying in his bed, engaged in conversation. We had been there since it was light out, and now darkness filled the room.

Despite spending a considerable amount of time together, we hadn't progressed beyond first base. So, I figured that was the perfect opportunity to push the boundaries.

I kissed his neck and whispered, "I'm going to do something, but don't ask me why, okay?"

He turned his mouth toward my ear and responded, "Go ahead."

Nervously, I traced my hand down his slender frame until I reached the buckle of his pants. I contemplated if I should continue on, but curiosity guided me a bit further.

I slipped my hand inside and roamed around until I discovered a hidden treasure, instantly bringing it to life.

"Now I have a question for you," David asked, a hint of amusement in his voice. "What are you doing down there?"

"Does a woman need a reason to caress her man?"

"Oh, that's what you're doing? It feels like you're playing with a toy."

I laughed, a little embarrassed about my lack of experience.

"How am I supposed to do it?" I asked softly.

David placed his hand on mine and gave me a little tutorial. Taking things a step further, he slowly traced his hand up my back and unclasped my bra.

Still uncertain of how far I was willing to go, one thing was clear — I wasn't stopping anytime soon.

However, as if she were clairvoyant, my mom thought otherwise. In the height of our little rendezvous, my beeper went off, interrupting the flow. I tried to ignore it, but moments later, it chirped again.

"Go ahead and check it," David said, sitting up in bed.

I glanced at the beeper, hoping it wasn't someone important. As soon as Faye's 911 flashed before my eyes, I knew it meant trouble. My heart raced as I grabbed the phone to call her back.

"Girl, your momma is blowing up my phone," she exclaimed. "I haven't answered because I know she's calling for you."

There we go again. Just as I started to feel like a woman, reality swooped in to remind me that I was a 17-year-old girl, forbidden from having a boyfriend, let alone being at his house after dark.

"Okay," I panicked, "I'm at David's house, but I'm on my way."

I hung up the phone and peeked in his direction. "Let me take a wild guess," he said, "your mom is looking for you."

I sighed and said, "Yes, I need to head over to Faye's house to call her back."

He buried his face in his hands, as if to convey, I'm too old for this childish game.

The ride to my cousin's house was devoid of conversation. While I can't speak for him, my mind was a whirlwind of thoughts. How did I go from having such a pleasant experience to enduring another embarrassing moment? The only solace I found was knowing that my eighteenth birthday was in three short months. Surely, I would be allowed to date then?

Upon arriving at Faye's house, I didn't immediately get out of the car. Instead, I sat for a while in the tension of the night. After a few moments, David spoke.

"I don't understand why some parents are so strict. I think it's a control issue," he said, flicking the door handle with his finger.

"What's bothersome is my sister was allowed to have a boyfriend when she was my age," I replied, trying to keep the conversation flowing.

"So, why do you have all these restrictions? Are you the problem child?"

"No, this is my step-dad's rule, and she's just following along."

"Have you considered moving with your dad?" he asked. "You might have more freedom over there."

I rested my head on David's shoulder and recounted my experience of living with my father.

"I moved in with my mom because I couldn't handle living with him anymore. He would get angry over the smallest matters. One night, he woke me up at 2 am just to find a spoon."

"A spoon?" He looked puzzled.

"Yes, a spoon. I was still rubbing sleep out of my eyes when I walked into the living room to find him standing in the kitchen, ranting about how careless I was. He also said that I would never amount to anything more than the tramp I walked around dressed like, and I would end up on welfare with a bunch of babies."

He put his hand over his mouth and laughed. "Damn, all that over a spoon? Was he drunk or something?"

"No, he doesn't drink or do drugs. I have no idea why he reacted that way over a missing spoon."

"Wow, that's crazy," he said, shaking his head.

"It's ridiculous, but you know what? Those words are ingrained in my mind, and I'm determined to prove him wrong. That's why I'm still a virgin. I can't risk getting pregnant and proving him right."

Silence filled the air, as if someone suddenly muted the sound. I had been waiting for the perfect time to drop the 'virgin bomb' because, surprisingly, he never asked.

"So, your dad went ballistic over a spoon, huh?" he stated, reverting the conversation. "Was it his favorite spoon or something?"

"Actually, we only had two. But he couldn't find the other spoon either." We burst into laughter, but our enjoyment was cut short by the sound Faye tapping on the window. "Your mom is on the phone, and she is upset."

"Back to reality," I mumbled, as I exited the car and rushed to the phone. I knew I would have to do some hard convincing. Luckily, I had become quite good at it.

"Did you ask my permission to leave this house!" she yelled the moment I picked up the phone.

"I left you a note that I was coming to Faye's house," I said, as innocently as possible.

"This note business is about to stop. If you don't get my permission first, then you don't leave this house. Do you understand me? You think I haven't noticed that you've been on the go every weekend? I better not find out that you're messing around with some boy."

"I'm not with a boy. I came over here with Faye because I was bored at home alone."

"Well, as I said before, I never gave you permission to go over there. You better come home, now!" She hung up without another word.

I turned to Faye with tears in my eyes. "Can you please take me home? I would ask David, but she'll probably be watching." She agreed, but I could sense that she wasn't happy with the entire situation.

I went outside to inform David that our evening had officially come to an end. "Faye has to drive me home. I'm sorry, I ruined our night," I said, feeling like a kid.

"You didn't ruin our night. Your mom tried, but I actually enjoyed sitting here talking to you."

"Me too," I smiled, as I leaned in for a kiss.

"You know what else I enjoyed? Feeling these little things right here," he said, putting his hand up my shirt.

"Little? Whatever, I have some huge breasts. They are triple D's."

"Okay, Ms. Triple D. You better head home before your mom comes to get you."

We kissed once more before parting ways. I was certain my mom would argue all night, but in my heart, it was worth it. However, much to my surprise, when we arrived at my house, everything was completely dark.

"That's messed up," Faye commented. "She made you come home and they're probably out for the night." I shook my head in disbelief, thankful it would all be over in a few short months.

After I turned in for the night, I called David but his grandmother said he wasn't home. 'Hmm, I wonder where he could be?' I closed my eyes, and happily relived the magical moment that took place in his bed just a few hours earlier.

Back to Reality

Startled by King's crying, I was jolted back to reality. The harsh reality was—my dad was right. I did end up on welfare with a bunch of babies. How could he have known?

As I prepared King's bottle, I looked around at the place I called home. The only pieces of furniture that adorned the living room were a dining table my mom gifted me, and a high chair. The rest of the large, empty space was just carpet and walls, which had red streaks from a permanent marker Kevin managed to get a hold of.

Staring at the red lines scribbled across the room, the answer became painfully clear. How did I end up here: Because of love, or a lack thereof?

I loved David so much that I justified his mistreatment; I ignored all the rumors about other women, and I didn't insist on him using protection because he got upset whenever I'd ask. I just wanted to be with him and nothing else mattered.

"But where is he now?" I pondered. "Lately, he hasn't been around. He helped me get this apartment after the twins were born, but it's too expensive. I had to sell all my furniture last month just to pay the rent. This isn't the scenario I envisioned when I moved so far away from my family. I thought this would be the start of our new family. Instead, I'm all alone on my twenty-third birthday with a baby who cries all day long."

As the sound of King's crying intensified, I opened the cabinet and took out a bottle of Nyquil. I glared at the red liquid inside and considered adding just a few drops to his bottle. "Naw, I can't give him this." I left the bottle on the counter and went back into the bedroom.

"Happy birthday to me," I whispered, as I took my toddler into my arms, and rocked him back and forth. Once he drifted off to sleep, I lay my head on the pillow and continued to recount the events in my life that led up to that day.

Chapter 4

The Writing on the Wall

t was the summer of 1998. As a recent graduate, I felt it was time to board one of those planes I had been so obsessed with watching soar high in the sky. For my summer vacation, I went to visit my eldest sister Rita and her husband, who lived in Texas.

This was going to be a summer of many firsts: the first time I got on a plane, my first-time leaving Florida, and the first time I would be away from David for an extended period. It had been four months since our paths crossed that great day in March, and we managed to spend time together consistently ever since.

I was excited to visit my sister, but even more excited about returning home a week before my eighteenth birthday. This meant I was on the fast track towards freedom! I would soon be able to date without having to plot and scheme. After four months, it had become exhausting, especially with my mom assuming the role of a private eye.

One day, she found my beeper and forced me to sell it to my friend. In return, I secretly bought it back from her a couple of days later in school.

I felt relief knowing all those days were about to become a thing of the past!

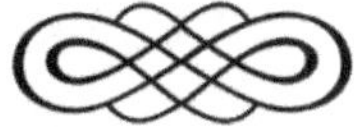

My time in San Antonio with Rita and her family was delightful. We visited Six Flags, the River Walk, and attended a military house party, among other things. Nonetheless, after being away for two weeks, I was starting to get homesick for one person in particular.

I tried contacting him several times, with no success. Finally, one evening, I managed to catch him at home. "Where have you been?" I questioned the moment David answered the phone.

"Well, hello there," he replied. "I've been working overtime to keep busy while you're away. Remind me, when are you coming back?"

"This Saturday, and I can't wait to see you."

"So, I'll pick you up from the airport?" he suggested.

"Um… my flight gets in late, and my mom is picking me up," I said hesitantly.

He paused and I knew that meant trouble. "Now that you've graduated, we don't have to sneak around anymore, right?"

"That's correct, and besides, I'll be leaving for the Navy in a couple of weeks," I affirmed.

"I know you're leaving, young lady. You don't have to keep telling me."

I made the decision to enlist in the military at the start of my senior year, before that fateful day in March when David and I met. Despite my strong feelings for him, I wasn't willing to change my plans just to be with him; no matter how far my head was in the clouds, I remained keenly aware of my priorities, with the top one being, to prove my dad wrong at all costs.

"Yeah, okay," he added. "I'll see you when you get back."

"You sure will!" I attempted to lighten the mood, but the call ended on a sour note.

"He doesn't sound too happy. I'll have to make it up to him when I get home."

The Writing on the Wall

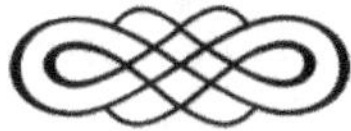

The plane ride back was very serene. Once I got over the fear of plummeting to my death, I found myself actually enjoying the experience of flying the friendly skies.

Gazing out at the sunset and appreciating the beauty of life, I regained my excitement about leaving for the Navy. Now, the lingering question remained: should I sleep with David before I left?

Despite spending a significant amount of time together, my virginity remained intact. Primarily because our happy relationship wasn't as blissful as it appeared.

On several occasions, he would disappear, providing various excuses about his whereabouts when I asked. Additionally, he had a strong connection with his daughter's mother which was unsettling. He often reminisced about their high school days and how she was his first love, yet I refrained from questioning it, fearing I would sound insecure.

Then there was his God-sister, Linda, who lived just around the corner from him and frequently borrowed his car. She had a daughter the same age as David's, and they attended private school together. When I questioned why he helped her so much, he explained that they grew up together, and she was like family.

Although I hadn't officially met her, she held such a significant role in his life that I felt like I knew her. Until one day I waved as she drove by in his car when I got off the bus. The puzzled look on her face quickly reminded me that we had never been introduced.

Oddly enough, I was always in his room when she stopped by. However, after that awkward encounter with Ebony, I was perfectly fine without meeting any more of his female friends.

As the plane soared through the night sky, I closed the window shade and turned my thoughts toward our failed attempt at intimacy, and his peculiar behavior the following day.

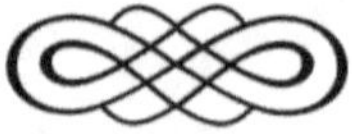

One weekend, I went over to Faye's house while she was at work. Knowing everyone would be gone, I thought it would be perfect to spend time alone with David and finish what we started that steamy night in his bed. At least, that was the plan. However, several hours later, everyone had returned home, and David still hadn't shown up.

That wasn't the first time he had left me hanging, and I was growing quite tired of it.

Another incident happened the night of my prom. After my mom imposed tight restrictions on what I could wear and who I could go with, I decided to forego the prom and spend the evening with the new love of my life.

The agreement was that he would take his daughter to her mom's house and then pick me up afterwards.

On the contrary, he never returned, never called, and I spent the entire night sitting on Faye's couch, waiting for him to show up like a little girl waiting on her unreliable father.

The following day, he explained that he'd been detained by the police while they searched his car for hours. When I asked why he didn't at least call, he justified it by saying he was too upset to talk. "Well, that makes two of us," was all I could muster in response.

But this particular weekend, I was prepared to let him have it. How dare he stand me up, after I had to lie and sneak just to be with him?

My cousin Faye was down to earth, but my mom's intuition was right; the only reason I went over there so much was indeed to spend time with 'some boy.' Otherwise, I would have stayed home most weekends.

I decided to call it a night when the doorbell rang. Well, well, Mr. Hall had finally made an appearance, only ten hours late. I swung the door open and stepped outside.

"I can't believe you kept me waiting the entire day. It's almost midnight!" I yelled.

"I'm sorry, but it's my grandma's birthday and I forget we had plans to take her out," he explained.

"And once again, you couldn't call?" I crossed my arms and rolled my eyes.

"Don't roll your eyes at me, young lady. No one is more important than my grandma. If you can't respect that, then I have nothing more to say to you," he said, with a sternness that caused my courage to retreat. I noticed that whenever he got upset, his words turned cold and harsh.

"I'm just saying, I came over here for us. Instead, I spent the entire day alone."

"I'm here now. So, are you going to be sour all night?" he said, pulling me close.

Who was I fooling? I couldn't remain angry with him, and he knew it. Truth be told, I was just happy he showed up at all, no matter how many hours late.

"Let's sit on your car," I said, having decided to carry out my original plan.

We walked over, and I hopped on the hood. Taking hold of his hand, I examined his nails to make sure they were clean. "You can't find anything better to do with your hand?" I asked, playfully rubbing his fingers.

"Like what?" he smirked.

"Maybe you should put it someplace warm," I smiled mischievously.

I couldn't tell if he was simply respectful of my virginity, but I found it strange that I was usually the initiator of any advances between us.

"Wow, your nails are getting long," I said, distracted by the length of his pinky nail.

"I keep the pinky and thumb nails long to cut open boxes at work. But getting back to what you were saying, where did you want me to place my hand?" he smirked, once more.

"I can show you better than I can tell you." I took his hand and guided it underneath my skirt.

David stared into my eyes as his fingers began to roam. Returning his stare, I moved toward the edge of the car, inviting him to go further. He obliged, and I closed my eyes, enjoying the sensation.

Just like that, my frustration about him not showing up on time or inviting me to his grandmother's birthday celebration dissipated. Instead, I felt fortunate that the man I didn't feel worthy of dating still chose to date me.

My blissful thoughts were interrupted by the sound of David unzipping his pants. My eyes popped open. 'Does he really think we're about to have sex?' I wanted to fool around since we hadn't done more than kiss since that night at his house, but sex was definitely not on the agenda.

My mind scrambled as I contemplated what to do next. I didn't want to ruin the moment, but there was no way my first time was happening in the front yard of my cousin's house. To add to the discomfort, it had been raining all day and the mosquitoes were starting to attack.

David sensed my hesitation and softly put his lips on mine. Then he slowly moved to my neck, and I lost all train of thought.

It quickly returned when he grabbed my hips and forcefully pulled me closer. "What are you doing?" I asked, in a panic.

"Just relax; I'm not going all the way."

"Yeah, that's what they all say."

"Are you going to relax and enjoy this, or what?" he stated, already continuing his pursuit.

I tried to relax, but how could I? My first time was about to happen outside on the hood of a car. 'I waited nearly eighteen years for this moment, and it's happening like this?' was my frantic thought.

My eyes were starting to water, when I heard the most harmonious sound escape from David's lips. "Ouch!" he exclaimed, slapping his leg. "These mosquitoes are having me for dinner."

He stepped back and zipped his pants.

'Thank you, God, for every mosquito that invaded this yard, on this day,' was all I could think as I jumped down from the hood of his car.

"Is your cousin still up?" he asked.

"How about we head back to your house?" I suggested, thinking it would be more romantic there.

"Actually, I just remembered I have to take my uncle home. His car broke down."

"You're leaving already?" I said, my disappointment evident.

"Sorry, but I have to go. Are you going to be here tomorrow?"

"Faye has to work, but I'll stay if you're coming back."

"Sure, I'll come over after I drop my daughter off."

"Please show up this time," I pleaded.

"I will young lady, I will."

What a Difference a Day Makes

Sleep eluded me the entire night. Instead, I was wide awake, filled with anticipation for what awaited me in the morning. "What if it's too painful? What if I get pregnant? I would make sure he used protection."

My thoughts drifted to the night the pastor's son tried to guide me into womanhood. It was a Wednesday night, and my parents were at Bible study. He stopped by, and for the first time I invited him inside. I even gave him a tour of the house, inevitably leading to my bedroom—a bold move, I must admit.

Even though our time together was limited, my feelings for him were genuine. We talked on the phone most evenings while he worked the late shift, sharing laughs and engaging in meaningful conversation. Above all, he treated me with the utmost kindness and respect.

I'll never forget the first kiss we shared in my driveway (which was actually my first French kiss). I giggled at the thought of my parents pulling up and seeing us there, especially since we both were playing hooky from church.

Looking into his eyes and feeling his embrace, I tuned out my surroundings as our lips touched under the moonlight. As I walked away, he called my name. I turned and he asked, "Can I have some more?" My heart melted.

Certainly, I would have loved for him to be my first. The night of our little house tour, I was all set to take things to the next level. Unfortunately, or maybe fortunately, that plan hit a roadblock. No matter how hard I tried to relax, access wasn't easily granted; after a couple of failed attempts, we agreed to try again later, fearing my parents might return.

Now, lying awake and counting down the hours until David's return, I wondered whether "entry" would also be an issue for him. A whirlwind of thoughts flooded my mind, all of which would be answered by the ringing of Faye's doorbell in a few short hours... or so I thought.

The next morning, David showed up as promised, but there was something peculiar about his demeanor. I was all fired up, but he didn't share the same level of enthusiasm.

We sat in silence on the couch until I took the initiative, once again. I leaned over to kiss him, but to my surprise, he turned away.

"Chill out, I'm trying to watch TV," he responded.

I glanced at the program idly playing on the screen, and thought, 'Is this dude serious? Last night, he was ready to have sex on the hood of his car. Now, with ample time and opportunity, he prefers to watch television?'

I rested my head on his lap, hoping that might lighten the mood, but instead, I caught a whiff of something unpleasant.

My head popped up just as swiftly as it went down. 'Is that the reason he's acting like this, because he didn't take a shower? I don't understand him. He's supposed to be all over me right now, instead he sits here in smelly silence.'

"Hey, I'm about to head home," he stood up and walked to the door.

"What do you mean, you just got here?" I said, confused.

"Sorry, but I have something I need to take care of."

"Okay, but you're coming back, right? You're supposed to spend the day with me, remember?"

David opened the door, exposing the bright sunlight. "I never promised to spend the day with you. I said I'd swing by after dropping off my daughter to her mom's, and I did. Now, I have something I need to take care of."

Feeling rejected once more, I just stood there at a loss for words.

He stepped outside, and then turned to face me. "I'll call you later. Are you going to be here tonight?"

"Why would I stay here all day for nothing? I'm going home!" I slammed the door.

GOOD ON PAPER GUY

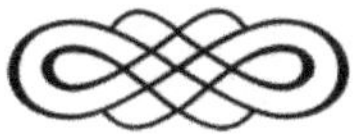

How could he be exactly what I wanted
but nothing that I needed him to be?

Giving me everything
yet nothing at all

How could tender kisses in the night
leave me empty in the light?

He showers me with his love
yet, I'm still longing

Longing for that perfect touch
that will melt this ice away

Fantasy guy come to life
but the reality, not so great

I have a thirst he can't quench
a hunger he can't satisfy

Always wanting more, more than he can give
Wishing he was my soul mate
but it feels like we're worlds apart

How could he be good on paper

but not in my heart?

CHAPTER 5

PARENTS JUST DON'T UNDERSTAND

"**N**ow that you are about to turn eighteen, you can start dating if you want," my mom said, as we rode home from the airport.

I was shocked. I couldn't believe she was granting my heart's desire so freely. The entire time I was in Texas, I had been rehearsing my 'I should be free to date' speech.

"Is there anyone in particular that you want us to meet?" she asked.

Hmm, perhaps this is a trick. Maybe she's trying to confirm her suspicion that I've been sneaking around all this time?

"Yes, there's this guy I met named David." I decided to forge ahead.

"David, huh? And how old is he?"

"He's nineteen," I lied, afraid she would not approve of him being twenty-two.

"And how did you meet him?"

"At work," I confessed.

She stopped talking, and I knew the jig was up. I immediately prepared my speech with supporting facts to back it up.

"Alright, when do you plan to introduce him to us?" she continued.

My stomach fluttered. It's definitely a setup. "I have to check with him first, but perhaps Friday?" I figured the sooner they met, the sooner I gained my emancipation.

"Sounds like a plan. I'll let James know."

I maintained my composure, but internally, I was dancing in my seat. I was ecstatic and couldn't wait to tell David the good news.

Parents Just Don't Understand, Or Do They?

"Ugh, I'm not good at meeting parents," David grumbled into the phone.

"You'll do fine. Then we can spend time together without having to sneak around."

"I guess you're worth it," he said, mockingly.

"I sure am. So, I'll see you Friday night?"

"Yeah, yeah, I'll be there."

I eagerly waited for Friday the entire week. When it finally arrived, I wished it hadn't. From the moment David got there, James bombarded him with questions, most of which he couldn't answer:

"Do you have any career goals?"

"Not really."

"Where do you see yourself in five years?"

"I don't know. I pretty much live day-to-day."

"Do you have any kids?" James continued.

"Yes, a two-year-old daughter who lives with me."

"What are your intentions with my daughter?"

"Oh, we're just kickin it."

James's expression changed. "Just kickin it?"

I was also puzzled. I had presented him as my new boyfriend, and in just four words, he shattered that illusion.

James remained cordial, but didn't feel the need to continue his line of questioning. "Well, it was nice meeting you, young man. We plan on having a cookout before Sabrena leaves for the military, and we'd be happy to have you attend."

"Sounds good to me," David said.

My mom nodded in agreement. They all rose and shook hands before saying goodnight.

"He caught me off guard with those questions about my future," David said as we walked to his car. "I don't waste time worrying about what's going to happen five to ten years from now. I take life one day at a time.”

Sensing his uneasiness, I tried to reassure him that none of that mattered, at least not to me. “Don’t worry about those questions, James is known for being Heathcliff Huxtable. The only answer that confused me was, ‘we’re just kickin it.’ Why did you say that?”

I needed an explanation, because as the first boy I brought home, he made me look foolish in front of my parents.

As usual, David found a way to justify his actions. “I told them that for your benefit. Think about it, if I said you were my lady, it would’ve been obvious that you were sneaking around. I mean, how could we have just met and already be a couple?”

Well, that made sense. I still would’ve preferred him to tell the truth, but I figured it wasn’t a big deal, right?

Wrong... I was about to discover that it was a very big deal.

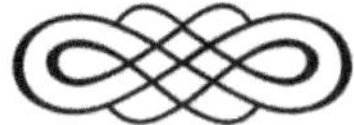

In the weeks that followed, I had to visit the Navy recruitment center every day to work out. I was still a few pounds over the weight limit and had to seriously buckle down before the official weigh-in.

By the end of the second week, I really missed spending time with David, so I invited him to stop by when I got home.

Given that I was officially allowed to date, I assumed it would be okay if we chilled outside for a while. Unfortunately, my mom felt otherwise.

I poked my head into the kitchen to let her know David had arrived and received a surprising response. "I know you didn't invite that boy over here this time of night," she said.

"This time of night? It's only eight o'clock."

"James and I are packing for our trip and we're not prepared to have company."

"Mom, he's not coming inside. We're just going to stand outside and talk."

"No, you're not! Now go out there and send him home."

'You have got to be kidding me?' I couldn't believe the words that were coming out of her mouth, and it showed on my face.

"I'm not playing with you, girl. And let this be your last time inviting him over here without my permission."

'I knew it was all a facade. Despite graduating from high school, enlisting in the military, and turning eighteen in two days, I'm still not allowed to stand in front of the house and talk to a boy. Unbelievable!' Reluctantly, I went outside to break the news to David that he had driven all that way for nothing.

"Hey, young lady, it feels like I haven't seen you in a month." He greeted me with a smile. "You've dropped some pounds, too. They must be working you hard down at that Navy center."

"Yes, they are. My whole body is sore."

He pulled me close. "I can help you out with that. Want to go back to my house for a massage?"

"I'd love to, but you wouldn't believe what just happened? I told my mom you were here, and she flipped out."

"Why? What's the problem?" he asked.

"I don't know; I told her you were staying outside, but she's reacting as if I invited you to dinner."

He frowned. "I knew your mom wouldn't allow you to start dating that easily."

"Also," I added, "she's making a big deal about you saying that we're just kickin it. I've overheard her discussing it on the phone multiple times."

Suddenly, James walked up the driveway. "Hello, young man. I don't know if Sabrena informed you, but her mom wants her in the house. We're going on a trip this weekend and aren't prepared to have company over this evening."

"No problem, I was just about to leave," David replied.

"As I mentioned the other day," James added, "we're planning a cookout, and we'll invite you over at that time. Sabrena, tell your company goodnight."

I acknowledged his words, but didn't move. "Tell your friend goodnight," he repeated. "You two are just friends, right?"

"It sounds like you don't believe us," David responded, though I wished he hadn't.

"Excuse me?" James turned back.

"It sounds like you think I'm lying. If that's how you feel, don't beat around the bush. Be a man and come out and ask me."

"What do you mean 'be a man'?" James raised his voice. "Don't stand in front of my house and question my manhood. No, I don't believe you were telling the truth. I think you're a low-life with questionable intentions towards my daughter!"

"Well, I'm sorry you feel that way, but why would I waste my time lying to you?"

James was fuming. "Who the hell do you think you're speaking to, son? I'll break you down to size."

'Dear God, please don't let them fight,' was all I could think.

Seeing the fear in my eyes, James took a deep breath to regain his composure. "Young man, you're not allowed back at my house. Sabrena, let's leave right now." I whispered goodnight, and quickly walked away.

Taking a few steps, I glanced back to see David's reaction and noticed him chuckling as he got into the car. 'Does he really think this is funny?' I was disturbed.

I entered the house to find James recounting the events to my mom. "Where is he?" She marched toward the door. "I sent you out there. Let him talk that mess to me," she huffed.

"He already left, baby," James said.

"Oh, because I was about to give him a piece of my mind. Talking about they're just kickin it. Well, he'll have to 'kick it' with somebody else because you're not allowed to see him again; do you hear me?" she said, glaring angrily in my direction.

"But we are just friends." Now, I was trying to sell them on the lie.

"Not anymore, you're not!" She wagged her finger in my face. "Your birthday is in two days, and you can forget about going out with him."

Fed up with her dictatorship, I opened my mouth and spoke. "You can't forbid me from having a boyfriend anymore. I'm turning eighteen."

The instant the words left my mouth, I wanted to retract them, especially after she snapped and began hitting me with the hangers she was holding. I raised my arm to shield myself, but she just went wild.

"Don't tell me you're turning eighteen. After all I've done for you, you think you can give me your behind to kiss for some boy who cares nothing about you?"

"He does care about me!" I yelled, in tears.

"Oh really? A respectful boy would've come here and said, I like your daughter, and I'd like to date her."

'What was this, the 1960s? Guys don't do that anymore, and why should he? None of my friends had to jump through all these hoops just to have a boyfriend. It's not like he was asking for my hand in marriage.'

"Everybody just needs to calm down," James intervened. He was always the voice of reason.

"Sabrena, you seem very emotional about this young man. It's hard for me to believe you two just met or that you're only friends. However, let me offer this piece of advice—you don't want to be with someone who doesn't show respect to your parents. That speaks volumes about his character."

I remained silent, neither agreeing or disagreeing with his statement.

"You can date him if you want, but he disrespected me at my house, and he is not allowed back over here," James concluded.

"She's not allowed to date him, and that's final," my mom huffed. "Good thing you're leaving for the Navy because if you continue 'kickin it' with him, you'll end up on welfare with a house full of babies.

CHAPTER 6

THE GOOD SAMARITANS

My eyes popped open. There go those words again—on welfare with a bunch of babies. The very scenario I had fought so hard to avoid had indeed become my reality.

When the twins were born, my eldest was just 15 months old, making it feel more like I had triplets. Buying diapers, milk, and clothes for three babies at once was more than challenging. Some days, it felt downright impossible.

However, the difficulties didn't end there. My circumstances took a turn for the worse when I lost my position as a TSA agent due to poor attendance. With two babies keeping me up all night, working a 4 am shift was very taxing. Not to mention, I had to get all three of them up, dressed, and to the 24-hour daycare down the street by 3 am.

David rarely spent the night anymore, leaving me to fend for myself most days. He explained that he couldn't get any rest at my house. His response to my complaints was, "It wouldn't benefit either of us if I got fired too, would it?"

So, at the age of twenty-two, I assumed the role of an unmarried mother of three just as any girl would, with great shame.

I paid for additional hours at the daycare so they could attend seven days a week. Rarely did I take them out in public, and when I did, I kept my head down, avoiding eye contact with anyone who came near. I knew they were judging me, because deep down, I was judging myself.

THE GOOD SAMARITANS

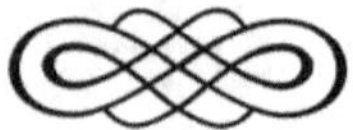

Three months into unemployment, my car was repossessed, and life just kept spiraling downward. I don't know what was worse—being without a car or having to catch the bus with a toddler and two infants.

To add to my dismay, the nearest bus stop was eight blocks away. Although getting to the bus stop wasn't the problem, I had this huge twin stroller that looked more like a bus itself. The real challenge was boarding the bus.

To accomplish this simple task, I had to take each child out of the stroller, find someone onboard who was willing to hold them (usually the person nearest to the door) and then get back off the bus to fold up the stroller. If that wasn't embarrassing enough, I then had to lug the stroller onto the bus, pay the driver, and collect my toddlers—all to the viewing pleasure of everyone onboard.

The process repeated itself when it was time to get off the bus, only by then, there were even more watchful eyes.

Needless to say, I loathed taking the bus and enduring the entire stroller ordeal. One day, I had the bright idea to leave the stroller at home. I thought it would make my plight much easier if Kevin walked while I carried the twins.

So, with Katie in one arm and King in the other, we began our eight-block hike to the bus stop. It started out fine, but slowly unraveled around the fifth block when Kevin began to cry.

"Mommy, my feet hurt," he whined.

"Keep walking, baby; we are almost there."

We took a few more steps, and Katie began to slip out of my arms. I had to press her against my side to keep her from falling. I must have pressed too hard because she began to cry, too.

Coming to a stop, I tried to push her back up with my knee. I could only imagine how I looked, standing there on the street, struggling with two babies in my arms, and a toddler crying beside me.

After I finally got Katie back in position, we continued our hike.

"Mommy, it hurts," Kevin whined, once more.

"There's the bus stop right over there. Come on, baby, keep walking," I urged.

"Noo!"

And just like that, he sat on the ground.

Glancing at the bus stop a couple of yards away, then back at Kevin, I had never felt so helpless and unsure of what to do next. Every part of me wanted to give up and sit on the ground, too.

"Excuse me, do you need a ride?" shouted a lady from the passenger window of a car that had pulled over.

I simply stared at her. Though I obviously needed help, I was skeptical about accepting a ride from complete strangers.

"We can give you a ride wherever you need to go. I have my baby in the back seat, too."

Realizing my options were limited, I agreed.

She and the male driver got out of the car and took the twins out of my arms. I picked Kevin up and got in the back seat. "Where are you headed?" the driver asked.

"I was heading to the bus stop; it's right over there."

"No, I mean, what is your actual destination?"

"Yeah, we can take you wherever you need to go," the female passenger chimed in. "We don't have any plans today. We were just going to the store."

"I was taking them to the daycare further up the road.

You can just drop us off there, and I'll be fine."

"Sounds good. I'm Amanda, by the way, and this is my husband, Charles."

"I'm Sabrena. Thanks for giving me a ride."

"No problem at all. We saw you struggling with those babies in your arms and wanted to help you out."

Tears instantly filled my eyes. I was ashamed.

"You don't have a stroller for them?" Charles asked.

Looking away, I replied, "Yes, but I have a hard time getting it on the bus. I thought it would be easier if I walked to the bus stop without it, but apparently not."

"Aw, they are so cute. How old are they?" Amanda asked, while rubbing Katie's hand.

"My twins are ten months, and my son just turned two."

"Oh, they're twins! What a blessing!"

I locked eyes with her and fought the urge to say, "It doesn't feel that way."

Noticing my expression, she turned back around.

I peeked over at her son sitting in his car seat eating Cheerios; he was so adorable to me. Why couldn't I feel that way about my own kids?

I looked at Amanda and Charles holding hands in the front seat and grew even more despondent. 'Why couldn't David be here with us like he was supposed to be?' Tears began to fall.

When we arrived at the daycare, Amanda helped me out of the car. "Here's my number," she said, handing me her business card. "We live in this area; if you need any help at all, feel free to call."

I thanked them as they departed, feeling a mixture of gratitude and skepticism. 'She was only trying to be nice. She doesn't want some poor black girl with a bunch of babies calling her phone.'

I tossed the card in the garbage and walked away.

Captain of My Ship, Master of My Destiny

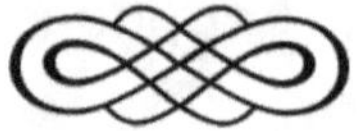

I am floating...
floating along life's river
looking for something
but going nowhere

Longing to be more than I am

I am captain of a ship
with no one on board
Master of a destiny
with no destination in sight

Standing above myself
looking down on myself
Visioning the me I want to be
yet not knowing how to become
all that I already am

Going nowhere
But wanting to be somewhere

Something...
Anything...

Captain of My Ship
Master of My Destiny

Chapter 7

The Aftermath

The next morning after David's encounter with James, I woke to find my mom on the phone, recounting the event to anyone who would listen. "He better be glad I wasn't out there. Talking about they're just kickin it. Well, she better find someone else to 'kick it' with on her birthday because it won't be him."

'That's what she thinks.' I went back to my room and closed the door. 'I'm celebrating my birthday with my man, and that's final.'

With a heart full of determination, I meticulously devised an escape plan and waited for the opportunity to carry it out.

Around 2 pm she called out to me from the living room. "We'll be back later, and you better not even think about calling that boy to come over here. Matter of fact, I'm going to tell Janet next door to keep an eye out."

James remained silent. I'd like to believe it's because he understood how I was feeling, unlike my mom, who took this on as her personal vendetta.

Once the coast was clear, I sat at the kitchen table and waited for enough time to pass before proceeding with my plan. Thirty minutes later, I grabbed the duffle bag I had secretly packed throughout the day, took out the bus schedule, and checked the time for the next bus. Only ten minutes to walk eight blocks; I had to make it.

After taking one last look around, I placed the letter I wrote my mom on the table. Heeding her warning about having Janet keep watch, I left out the back door and walked through the grass until I reached the end of the block.

My heart pounded as I hiked up the back street. Nervous yet determined, I refused to be treated like a kid any longer.

'Why can't I date whoever I please?' I thought angrily. 'After feeling like I've been on the outside looking in my entire life, I'm finally in a relationship with a guy who can have any girl he wants, yet he chose me, and she wants to take that away?'

I reached the corner just as the bus crossed the light. I had to dash for it, but I made it. Breathless, I boarded the bus, sank into the seat and closed my eyes.

Who would've thought I'd run away from home two days before my eighteenth birthday… but that's exactly what I did.

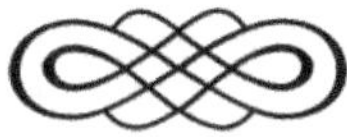

As soon as I arrived at Faye's house, I called David, and he came over. He was excited to hear that I had run away. In fact, Faye and her boyfriend Ben seemed excited, too. Ben had a similar run-in with James when Faye was in high school, so this was all very amusing to them. We joked and laughed about it, but after David left, reality set in. The reality was, I had left home and was now staying with my cousin. I traded the comfort of my room for a spot on her couch.

I checked the time and it was almost midnight. My mom had to be home, so why hadn't she called? I wondered if she read my letter and understood my point of view. Despite my efforts to sound sincere, I knew she wouldn't understand. I turned off the light and went to sleep.

The next morning, I woke up with a head full of thoughts. I checked the caller ID for any missed calls, but there were none listed. Later in the day, I decided to ask Ben to take me home to get the rest of my things.

I wasn't sure what was going to happen, but I couldn't handle the suspense.

When I walked into the house, she was in the kitchen on the phone (talking about me, no doubt). "I just came to get the rest of my stuff," I said, softly.

She glanced in my direction and resumed her conversation. Quietly, I slipped into the room to retrieve my belongings. When I returned, she was standing near the door.

"So, you're taking the rest of your things to Faye's house?"

"Yes," I answered, avoiding eye contact.

"Well, make sure you leave the keys before you go."

I shook my head. Instead of apologizing for being so controlling that she drove me away, she requested the keys.

"I know you think I'm being hard on you, but I'm just trying to prevent you from making the same mistakes that I did," she finally confessed.

Understanding her own experiences with having children at a young age, I attempted to plead my case,

"I'm leaving soon. How could he ruin my life in just four weeks? I just don't understand why I can't be allowed to date like everyone else my age."

Her eyes filled with tears and my heart sank. I never intended to make her cry.

"Alright," she relented. "If you want to date him that's up to you, but he has disrespected my husband and is not welcome at our house. I'll let you decide if you want to come home or stay over there with Faye and Ben."

"Okay," I said softly.

"In case I don't see you tomorrow, Happy Birthday."

She gave me a hug as tears streamed down her face.

"I love you, Mom."

"I love you, too."

On the ride back to Faye's house, I had a moment of truth: Was David truly worth all this turmoil? It seemed my appreciation for being with him stemmed more from my own insecurities than from his exceptional qualities. One thing was clear—I wasn't going to spend my remaining weeks in town waiting for him to show up while I sat alone on Faye's couch.

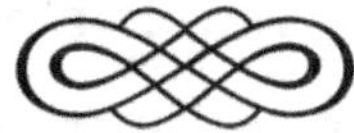

It was my eighteenth birthday! I had decided to go back home, but first, I was going to enjoy my special day. And I must say, this time Mr. David Hall did not disappoint. He showed up on time for our date, bearing flowers, a gift, and a smile.

Faye beamed as I left the house, all dolled up for my night out. "Don't wait up," I joked. It felt liberating to utter those words.

We went to dinner at Red Lobster, watched a movie, and then made our way to the beach. I've always loved the beach, but being there with David made it incredibly romantic. We settled on the stairs of the lifeguard tower and snuggled beneath the stars.

"The moonlight over the water is beautiful," I whispered.

"Yeah, this is exactly how it'll be the night I propose to you," he said.

I closed my eyes, sealing those words into my memory. "Mmm, the wind is blowing and the waves are crashing. I'm about to fall asleep."

"Oh yeah, let me see if I can wake you up." David turned my face towards him and kissed me ever so gently, sending shivers through me.

As we sat there, embracing in the moonlit night, I was certain that night was going to be special.

"You ready to become a woman?" he whispered.

"I thought I already was a woman."

"Not yet, but we can solve that problem right now." He stood up and took my hand. "Come on, let's lie in the sand."

I scanned the area, checking for others on the beach. I spotted a couple off in the distance, but it seemed they were already engaged in the same activity we were about to partake.

"Lie down on your stomach," David instructed.

"On my stomach, how is that going to work?"

"See, I told you that you weren't a woman yet."

I hated when he spoke to me that way. Besides, we didn't have a blanket. Was he expecting me to put my face in the sand?

"I don't want sand on my face. Why can't I just lie on my back?" I asked.

"Because it's easier to remove sand from your face than from your hair."

I suppose that made sense. I still wasn't entirely sure how it was going to work, but I decided to go along with it.

Shielding my face with my arms, I lay flat in the sand as he started things off with a gentle massage. "Ooh, now we're talking," I joked.

He kissed me softly and then paused. Without turning to look, I could hear the faint sound of paper tearing. 'This is it! It's finally about to happen and on a moonlit beach, no less. It's going to be perfect.'

So, I thought... despite multiple attempts, he could not close the deal. Eventually, I maneuvered from underneath him and sat up in the sand.

"This isn't working. We should try it the normal way," I suggested.

David frowned. "Let's just forget about it."

"No, I want this for us, but why can't I lie on my back?"

"It's your first time. It's going to hurt from any position. I don't understand why you can't endure a little pain and keep going. No woman has ever died while losing her virginity, but knowing you, you'd probably be the first," he said, sarcastically.

"That's not funny." I was suddenly no longer in the mood.

"You kind of killed the mood," he said.

"I was just thinking the same thing about you." I looked away.

David sat down and bumped me slightly with his shoulder. In return, I playfully tossed sand in his direction.

"Oh, you want a sand fight, huh?"

"Bring it on," I challenged, grabbing a handful.

Without hesitation, we dove into an all-out sand war, covering us both in powdery white. I couldn't contain my laughter as we rolled around on the ground, carefree.

I loved when he shed that tough-guy exterior and allowed the real him to shine through. That was the man I had grown to love—the one who made a habit of picking me up from work every evening because he didn't want me riding the bus after dark; the man whose arms I snuggled in after school as he shared stories about his life, and the man who respected my decision to wait, never pressuring me into intimacy before I was ready.

Somewhere in the midst of my admiration, he managed to pin me down long enough to cleverly make another attempt. It was so unexpected that I grabbed his shirt and closed my eyes.

He proceeded to ask those little questions that every guy feels the need to ask. I like to call them the courtesy questions:

"Are you alright?"

"Umm, hmm"

"You want me to stop?"

"Ugh, Ugh"

“Are you sure?”

“Yes.”

And just like that, I was welcomed into womanhood! As our moment came to an end, he kindly helped me up from the ground. I was covered in sand from head to toe, even in places where the sun doesn't shine.

I walked back to the car in a daze; I couldn't believe it finally happened. Glancing at David, I wondered if the moment meant as much to him as it did to me. The look of contentment on his face suggested that it might have.

A New Day Dawning

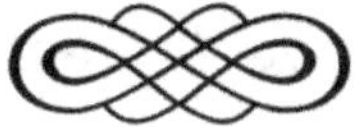

The next couple of weeks seemed to fly by. I moved back home, and David was upset. Although I reassured him that things would be different, he didn't approve. As a result, he became distant and was never available whenever I called. It was disappointing not to spend my final weeks with him, but reconciling with my mom took precedence. Even as a teenager, I had a God-consciousness that kept me from straying too far off track.

As the time drew near for my departure, I asked Faye to deliver a message to David at work. Finally, on my last day in town, he returned my call and made plans to see that evening.

Naturally reverting back to my usual routine, I told my mom that I was going over to Faye's house, and he picked me up at the corner.

"It sure doesn't feel like things have changed. It appears we're back to sneaking around," he remarked as I got in the car.

"Is that why I haven't heard from you in two weeks?"

"Yeah, pretty much. I've never been one for sneaking around. Not even when I was a teenager, so why start now?"

Determined not to argue with him on our final night, I settled in my seat and simply stared at the man I once found incredibly captivating. When we first met, I found him effortlessly cool. My initial impression was, 'he even drives like a gangsta,' when I saw him maneuvering with one arm on the steering wheel and the other leaning on the door. However, I later discovered the true reason behind his 'gangsta lean.'

One day, he made a sharp turn, and the door flew open. It turned out the door was broken, and he had to lean while driving to hold it closed. Sensing his embarrassment as he explained what happened to the door, I stifled my laughter until I made it home.

In that moment, I realized I was becoming increasingly disillusioned with my mystery man, even though much of the mystery remained.

Despite the rocky start, the evening turned out pleasant enough. Instead of repeating our beach night activity, we spent time hanging out and playing cards with his uncle and his uncle's girlfriend until it was time for me to head back home.

It was past 11 pm, and knowing my folks had settled in for the night, I instructed David to drop me off in front of the house.

"I'm going to miss you," I said, as we leaned against the car.

"No, you won't. You're going to forget all about me."

"How could I ever forget my first love?"

"I thought you said the pastor's son was your first love?"

"I thought he was, but that was false love. Our love is real."

David's expression changed.

"I better leave from in front of your house before your dad comes out and beats me up."

I laughed. "Alright, give me one last kiss before you go."

As we gazed into each other's eyes, I still held a heart full of gratitude for the man who had allowed me into his world. We promised to write, and I assured him I would call as soon as I could.

He kissed me softly and whispered in my ear, "Go, be great."

I went into the house and sat on my bed. The day I fantasized about had finally arrived and the realization was surreal. Tomorrow, a new chapter begins!

No more standing on the porch watching planes fly by, imagining the lives of the passengers. I was going to be one of those passengers. I wasn't sure what the future held for me, but one thing was for certain —I was ready to live.

My Destiny

It beckons me...drawing me near
with an urgency
unlike anything I've ever felt
It's an emptiness
at the end of my day

A longing...

that not even the strongest touch can erase
It calls out to me...pulling me near

It's, it's

My Destiny

Chapter 8

A Different World

If life only turned out the way we planned, there would be no need for faith. No need to hear inspirational messages of the triumphant overcomer, if there were no unfortunate circumstances to overcome. Only a select few have the pleasure of floating through life on easy street, seemingly having everything they touch turn to gold. I think those people exist to keep the rest of us hopeful, inspired and humbly seeking God for an inkling of the same fate. However, I've come to find, when life doesn't unfold according to your plans, it's because God has a more purposeful plan just waiting to be revealed.

What can I say about my brief time in basic training? It was certainly an unforgettable experience. The first day was challenging; the Chief Petty Officer came on deck, prompting everyone to rush to attention. Having just opened my locker, I stood there with the lock dangling off my dog tag chain. As he made his way through the barracks, he suddenly stopped, locked eyes with me, and yelled, "Put that shit away!" Shaken, I swiftly tucked the chain, along with the lock, inside my shirt.

Fortunately, my recruiter had given me the rundown on what to expect during basic training. "Remember, it's all a mind game. Don't take it personally, and you will be just fine," he cautioned.

Those words provided solace during the most challenging times, particularly the night when the fire alarm went off repeatedly, forcing us to run outside in 20- degree weather, wrapped in blankets. After the third alarm, I refused to get up. "Forget this; I'm not going back out there," I boldly declared, unaware that refusing to follow commands could land me in the brig.

Fortunately, God smiled on me that day because they declared it a false alarm, and everyone came back inside without anyone noticing that I had never left.

By the third week of training, I had found my stride. As a flag bearer, I assumed the leadership role in my line. I had grown accustomed to waking up at 4 am for breakfast, singing cadence while marching, and eye-flirting with guys in the next platoon.

I felt optimistic about my new world, though it became evident that not all recruits shared the same sentiments. Apparently, their recruiters hadn't been as honest about basic training as mine. They misrepresented the dynamics of boot camp, leaving several of my bunkmates shell-shocked. I couldn't help but chuckle to myself and think, 'I'm glad Petty Officer Bower kept it real with me.'

However, that all changed around the fourth week when it was time for the swim test.

Despite growing up in South Florida, surrounded by beaches and pools, I had never learned how to swim. So, when Petty Officer Bower first approached me about joining the Navy, I declined.

"I heard the Navy requires you to jump from a twelve-foot platform into deep water. I could never do that," I affirmed. "I'm afraid of heights and I can't swim."

"That's how they used to conduct the swim test back in the day, but it's different now," he explained. "You just have to tread water in a pool that's about five feet deep, and they'll guide you through it. Don't worry; you'll ace that swim test and sail around the world on a ship the size of a floating city. Japan, Germany, Europe —you'll get paid to visit all those places and more."

Those were the words that convinced me to join the United States Navy—the assurance of a minor swim test and the promise of world travel. So, you can imagine my shock when I turned the corner to enter the pool area and saw a twelve-foot platform with recruits stepping off into ten feet of water.

My eyes widened as I uttered the same words others had been saying for weeks: "My recruiter lied to me!"

Sure, there was a shallow end of the pool, but it was only used for a brief swim lesson before we were sent to the platform of doom.

Throughout my life, I had taken swim lessons, with no success. However, on this particular day, I made a single attempt to tread water and somehow managed to stay afloat for a few seconds without sinking. That brief accomplishment was enough for the officer to blow her whistle and declare, "Johnson, to the platform!"

With my heart racing, lips trembling, and my mind set on doing harm to Petty Officer Bower, I made my way towards the deep end of the Olympic-sized pool.

"Stand in line until it's your turn to climb," the officer instructed.

"I don't know how to swim," I said, hoping he'd send me back for more lessons.

"Just cup the water and push down. You'll rise to the surface."

I had no clue what that meant, let alone how to execute it, but it was too late. The whistle blew, and it was my turn to ascend the twelve-foot platform.

Upon reaching the top, I found three lines of recruits. The instructions were straightforward: move to the edge of the platform, cross your arms over your chest, and step off at the sound of the whistle. Simple in theory, yet incredibly hard for me to execute.

When the whistle blew, the other recruits stepped off, but I remained.

"I would hate to throw you off of here," the officer said, "Just take a deep breath and step off."

As I stood there shaking in my bathing suit, he signaled for the next two recruits to step up. "I can't swim and I'm afraid of heights. Please don't make me do this," I pleaded.

The whistle blew once more; two recruits stepped off, I remained.

"Please don't push me," I pleaded once more.

"You see that flag on the wall?" he asked.

I looked straight ahead at the American flag pinned to the wall. "Yes, I see it."

"If you can't do it for yourself, then do it for your country."

I shot him a glance that expressed precisely how I felt about my country at that moment.

"Alright then, off you go." He grabbed my arm and flung me from the platform.

I screamed all the way down.

When I hit the water, 'cup and push,' played on repeat in my mind as I sank deeper into the ten-foot pool. Soon, those words transformed into, 'hold your breath and pray.'

Suddenly, I felt two hands pulling me upward. I thought it was my guardian angel, but it turned out to be Navy divers.

Once we emerged, they surrounded me, yelling obscenities as I struggled to get out of the water.

If that wasn't traumatic enough, I was directed to join the quitter's bench alongside the other recruits thrown from the platform that day.

Once there, a female officer paced back and forth, scolding us. "You're a disgrace to the US Navy! You'll get back up there and step off again until you can do it without being pushed," she yelled.

'So, this is how my life ends?' I thought to myself.

Making my way back to the platform, my hands shook as I reached for the ladder. "You, step to the edge of the pool," instructed the male officer.

"I was told to return to the platform."

"Just stand at the edge of the pool, cross your arms, and step off," he instructed once more.

Unless they miraculously drained five feet of water from the pool, I wasn't on board with that idea either.

"I can't swim. Please don't make me do it," I cried.

His face took on an expression I hadn't seen since my arrival at basic training: compassion. He tried to give me a quick swim lesson, which was similar to the instructions I had received prior. "Just form a cup with your hands like this and push down as you rise to the top."

The words 'cup and push' were back on repeat in my mind.

"You got it?" he asked.

With no fight left, I stepped to the edge of the pool, closed my eyes, and stepped off into the deep.

I tried to cup, to push, to rise to the top, but instead, I found myself sinking further.

Once more, a diver descended and pulled me back up. This time, my rescuer was a woman. Instead of directing me to the quitter's bench, she instructed me to float around the pool.

'Are these people delusional? It should be abundantly clear by now that I can't swim, float, or cup and push.'

"I don't know how to float," I stated softly.

She smiled and said, "Don't worry; I'll show you."

Reluctantly, I leaned back as she supported me from underneath and guided me along the edge of the pool.

"Where are you from?"

"Miami," I answered.

"And you don't know how to swim? How is that possible?" she chuckled.

"I've had lessons, but never could get the hang of it."

"Floating is all about mindset," she said, "Just relax, and it'll come naturally."

I tried to relax, but when I realized we had floated beyond the safety of the pool's edge, my nerves returned. 'What if she lets go?'

She continued to speak, but her words became muffled as "it's a trap," echoed loudly in my mind.

Nevertheless, I maintained my composure as we glided across the water. In the distance, I faintly heard another recruit scream, followed by a big splash. I dared not look up; instead, I closed my eyes and tuned out completely.

The next words I heard were music to my ears: "Alright, you've successfully crossed the pool," she announced.

I sat up and quickly reached for the ladder. Once out of the water, she approached and handed me a document. "Congratulations, Johnson. You've passed the swim, and don't have to repeat this process again," she winked.

I saluted, as she walked away.

Looking down at the paper, I smiled. I guess my holy angel was in the water after all.

According to the United States Navy, I am a certified swimmer. Unfortunately, that piece of misinformation came at a price.

In the days following my swimming ordeal, I began to notice changes in my motor skills. It started subtly; my fingers would curl up when I tried to hold my pencil in class. Then, as the Commanding Officer loudly pointed out, I could no longer march in a straight line.

"Where the hell are you going, Johnson?" he'd yell as I veered off to the side.

By the end of the second week, it became evident that something was seriously wrong, yet the Navy doctors couldn't determine the issue. Their standard prescription remained unchanged: "Maybe you're dehydrated. Drink more water."

After the water remedy proved ineffective, and I started to suffer from excruciating migraines, they concluded that I had a pre-existing medical condition (which never existed before) and discharged me from the United States Navy.

CHAPTER 9

THE CLINIC

To say I was depressed was an understatement. To say I was near suicidal was right on the money. I eased out of bed and looked down at King who was fast asleep.

'Had I followed through with my plan to have an abortion, this wouldn't be my reality,' I thought to myself.

But how could I? The trip to the abortion clinic was one of the lowest moments of my life, and also one that I would never forget.

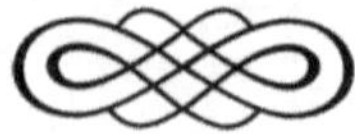

When David found out I was pregnant again, he was floored, particularly because Kevin was only five months old at the time.

"I'm already struggling to take care of my daughter and Kevin. Now you want to give me another mouth to feed?" he huffed into the phone.

"It's not like I planned this, David. You're the one who refuses to wear protection."

"You're the one who can't remember to take a simple birth control pill," he snapped.

"Yes, I forget sometimes, but I always remind you to wear protection, and you never do!" I shouted.

"Listen, the point I'm trying to make is we can't afford this right now," he softened his tone.

"Don't you think I'm aware of that? I'm only twenty-one; my life isn't supposed to turn out this way."

"So, how do you want to handle this?"

"I guess I'll get an abortion," I concluded, but the mere thought sickened me.

"Alright, find out how much it costs, and I'll take you on my day off," he said, abruptly ending the call without saying another word.

I took Kevin in my arms, the most adorable baby I'd ever seen, and logged onto the computer to find the nearest "Women's Clinic" in my area.

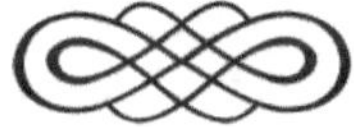

David pulled into the parking lot outside of Women's WellCare and turned off the engine. "You're not coming in with me?" I asked, nervously.

"We can't take Kevin in there. I'll just wait for you in the car."

I looked at Kevin, who was happily sucking on his toe and smiled, hoping that wouldn't be the last time I laid eyes on him.

I walked inside and provided my name to the receptionist, who directed me to change into a gown.

My heart instantly began to race. I'd heard stories about women who experienced complications while having an abortion, with some never waking up from the anesthesia.

I entered the dressing room and got undressed. The first gown had mildew stains, so I put it back and grabbed another one. "Lord, you know I can't handle two babies. I'm only twenty-one and I have so many dreams. Please see me through this, and I promise to never make this mistake again."

I walked out with my clothes in hand. "Put your things in the locker and have a seat in the waiting room," the nurse instructed.

As I made my way there, I passed a woman and a girl in the hallway. The girl was crying, and the woman was trying to comfort her, saying, "It'll be okay. It's not going to hurt, and I'll be right there with you."

I glanced at the girl and did a double take. She had ponytails in her hair and appeared no older than twelve. The nurse caught me staring and directed me to the waiting room.

When I walked in, there were three other girls waiting. The room was quiet save the sound coming from the television.

I sat in the nearest seat and glanced around the room. Everyone looked just as young as I was, but not nearly as young as the little girl in the hall. I couldn't help but wonder about her story. Did she get raped? Was it by someone she knew like a friend or a family member? I just couldn't conceive the thought of a little girl with ponytails having consensual sex.

"I hope this doctor hurries up," one girl said, finally breaking the silence.

"I know right," said another. "I came here yesterday, and he didn't even show up. The nurse said he had to deliver a baby. Now, where's the irony in that?"

They all laughed.

"I have to make it home before my boyfriend gets off from work," said the first girl. "He would be so mad if he knew what I was doing. He wants me to keep it, but I'm not ready for a baby. I'm only eighteen."

"At least he wants you to keep it. The guy I'm dealing with threatened to kick the baby out of my stomach if I don't get rid of it."

"Girl, you don't want to have a baby from somebody like that anyway. He sounds crazy. You better ask for a doctor's note to take home for proof," said the first girl.

Laughter filled the room once more, but I sat silently in my seat. I wasn't about to volunteer any information. Besides, how could they be laughing at a time like this?

"I already have one child and that's enough for me," the third girl chimed in. "I love my daughter to death and she is spoiled. She's not about to share her toys with another baby."

The room went silent.

"The doctor is here," the nurse announced. "I will call you one at a time, so get ready."

"I'm so scared," the first girl confessed. "That's why I've been talking so much; I hope nothing goes wrong."

I looked at her and saw fear in her eyes. I'm sure it was reflected in my eyes, too. Taking a deep breath, I said a silent prayer: 'God, I know this is against your will, but please see me through it. I promise I'll go back to church and get my life on track. Please don't let me die.'

"There's nothing to be afraid of," said the third girl. "This is my fifth one. It goes really fast and you don't feel a thing."

I stared at her in disbelief.

"Sabrena, you're up first," the nurse called.

Everyone watched as I walked into the exam room.

"Hello Sabrena," said the caramel-colored doctor, "You look nervous. Is this your first time?"

"Yes," I answered, timidly.

"There's no need to be afraid. I do about twenty of these a week and I haven't had any complications yet."

I found no comfort in his words.

"Lie down on the table and put your feet in the stirrups. We need to do a sonogram to get a better view of the fetus."

I climbed onto the table as instructed and turned my head. The sonogram screen was right next to me, and I didn't want to see a thing.

The nurse lubricated my stomach and moved the metal probe around until she found an image.

"Do you see what I see?" she asked the doctor.

"Yep, go ahead and inform her of her options while I make a quick phone call."

"My options?" I was confused. "Is there something wrong?"

"We have two issues: you're more advanced in your pregnancy than you initially stated, so the price has increased by a hundred dollars. You're also pregnant with twins, so that price is doubled."

"Twins! Are you sure?" I was shocked.

"Yes, I'm sure," said the nurse.

She placed the instrument back on my stomach and waited for the image to reappear. "Oh, look, that one is jumping around in here," she said with awkward excitement.

Instinctively, my head turned toward the screen, and she was right. There were two, and one of them was moving around. My eyes remained fixed on the image as she continued to speak. "You're about three months along, not two as you mentioned on the phone."

At that moment, the doctor returned. "So, what's your decision? The cost is now $1,200," he stated bluntly.

"I don't have $1,200," I said, still in shock.

"Then I suppose you'll have to come back another time. But don't wait too long because the price will only increase."

I returned to the dressing room and stood there as flashes of my babies went through my mind. 'Why was she jumping? She seemed so joyful. She....,' I glanced at the wall. 'How do I know it's a she? It could be a he. Two he's added to the one I already have.'

If the idea of having two babies scared me, the thought of three had me terrified. At that moment, I decided to explore adoption as an alternative because returning back to that clinic was out of the question.

Once I finished dressing, I walked out the door to deliver the news to David.

When I got in the car, he didn't say a word. My face was covered in tears, yet he remained silent.

The entire ride home, I grappled with how to tell him that not only did I decide against the abortion, but now we were expecting twins.

He pulled up outside my apartment and left the engine running. "You're not coming inside?" I asked, painfully aware of the answer.

"I have something I need to take care of," he stated as usual.

Disappointed, I pulled the money out of my pocket and tossed it into his lap.

"What's this?" He was puzzled.

"That's the abortion money. Thanks for asking how it went. Turns out, the price is now doubled because I'm three months pregnant with twins!"

Before he could respond, I got out of the car with Kevin and stormed off.

THE PRICE OF MY STONE

There's a price to pay for every brick
I lay on this path that's made of stone

Through sweat and tears and silent fears
I found the strength to press on

Overcoming my past, I've arrived at last
to a place I call my own

And when this path ends...
My Destiny Begins

For I have paid the price for my stone

CHAPTER 10

I ASKED, GOD ANSWERED

If you were to conduct an autopsy on every poor decision in your life, you would find that there was always a moment of truth: a crossroads where you had to choose between trusting God or yielding to the voice of your fears.

didn't want to raise three kids alone, or even one kid alone. I didn't want to be alone. Every instinct urged me to take the easy way out, to put the twins up for adoption and regain control of a life that was quickly spiraling out of control. I couldn't see my way clear.

However, after my mom showed me this heart-breaking story in the newspaper about a nine-year-old girl who was raped and murdered while in foster care, my plan to give them up for adoption went out the window. "Found naked in an alley outside the foster care, she was curled up in a fetal position like a baby put down to rest," the story read.

After hearing that, I couldn't bear the thought of subjecting my babies to the same fate. As a consequence, my relationship with David continued to deteriorate. He grew even more distant, and rumors about him and other women began to circulate.

One particular afternoon, I received a call from my cousin Faye. She and David still worked together. "Let me ask you something. Are you and David still together?" she inquired.

"Yes, why do you ask?"

"Because you're always calling the job for him and...," she paused.

"And what?" I asked, sensing her hesitation.

"Well, I wasn't going to say anything, but..."

"But what, Faye? Just say it," I pushed, growing agitated.

"Well, I heard this girl named Linda also has twins from him."

"What? No, Linda is his God-sister, and he's just helping her out," I said with certainty.

"His God-sister? Who told you that?"

"He did, and I believe him. She used to come to his house every morning and pick his daughter up for school."

"And he introduced her as his God-sister?" Faye questioned.

"Well, not officially. I used to be in the room when she stopped by, but my car was outside. I even dropped him off at her house before, so I know he's not sleeping with her."

The silence on the line was deafening.

"If you say so," she continued, "but he passed out cigars at work when her twins were born."

My heart sank. Not because I believed those were his twins, but because he didn't celebrate the birth of mine.

"Also," Faye added, though I really wished she wouldn't, "I heard that his daughter's mom had another baby from him, too."

I couldn't bear to listen to anymore, so I cut the conversation short. "Okay, Faye, I appreciate you letting me know what the rumors are."

"I'm only telling you because you're my cousin, and I care, but please don't repeat this to him. I don't want to be in the middle of any confusion," she requested.

"Yeah, sure," I agreed.

After we hung up, I sat there in a trance, reflecting on the day his daughter's mom gave birth. I was pregnant with Kevin at the time.

"My baby mama just had a little boy with the biggest feet," David said, as he walked in the door, smiling from ear to ear.

Admittedly, I was taken aback by his excitement. "I didn't know she was pregnant, and why were you at the hospital?"

"I took my daughter to see her little brother. Is that a problem?"

"No, I was just curious," I said, choosing to drop the issue rather than spoil our evening.

I've always had my suspicions about their situation, but I was confident that his God-sister, Linda, did not have twins from him. However, when he came over that evening, I confronted him about every allegation.

"How many kids do you have?" I grilled, the moment he walked through the door.

"Is that a trick question?"

"Just answer me, David," I demanded.

"Who do you think you're talking to?" He frowned.

"Faye told me that your daughter's mom had another baby from you. And that Linda has twins from you as well," I said, instantly repeating everything she shared.

David sighed. "Your cousin needs to get a life."

"Just answer my question!" I pushed.

He went into his pocket, and pulled out a keychain picture of Linda's twins. "Do you see any resemblance?"

Examining the two dark-skinned toddlers, I shook my head. "But, why are you carrying around a picture of her twins and not ours?"

"Did you give me a keychain picture of them? No, you didn't."

"And what about your daughter's mom?" I pressed further, "Is her son yours?"

"Hey, if you're going to believe every rumor you hear, then why are you with me?"

I lowered my head and replied, "I just don't understand why there are so many rumors about you."

David tenderly lifted my chin, locking eyes with me, he professed, "Sabrena, I have never cheated on you—not even once. I know I haven't been around lately, but I've been busy trying to make money to support you and the kids."

"But we barely have sex anymore," I said softly.

"I've been so stressed lately that sex is the last thing on my mind. After having three kids, I'm surprised it's even on yours."

"I'm only twenty-two, David. Of course, it's still on my mind."

He took me in his arms, and for the first time in a long while, kissed me passionately.

"Do you still love me?" he whispered.

"Of course I do."

Although, I couldn't explain why I loved him, but I did. At times, more than I loved myself.

He mistreated me, stayed away for days, and was incredibly rude whenever he got upset. Nevertheless, I still loved that man and held onto the hope that one day we would marry and have a stable family.

Unfortunately, or perhaps fortunately, I was about to discover that day would never come.

I Asked, God Answer

Waking up to the sound of King crying, I realized that my twenty-third birthday had come and gone, with no word from David. I spent the entire day alone, reflecting on my life, and questioning how things veered so far off track.

Without a clear answer, the only conclusion that emerged was the need to rekindle the flames with the man I loved. I firmly believed that our family could only be whole with him in the picture. Indeed, he was the missing piece to our puzzle.

Knowing he would eventually return so I could pick up Katie and Kevin, I got dressed and attempted to look my best— a challenging task most days.

Around noon, he finally strolled in. "I'm not in the mood to drive to your aunt's house. Take my car and go," David stated, as he took King out of my arms.

Thankful for a little freedom, I grabbed his keys and went out the door.

Driving to my aunt's house, I couldn't shake this overwhelming feeling of uneasiness. It dawned on me that even after six years together, David remained a mystery, though it was no longer alluring.

Upon returning home, I sat in the car. I recalled the day I told him that I had prayed and asked God if he was the right man for me. His expression changed, much like it did that night when I professed that our love was real.

With that in mind, I took a deep breath and opened his glove compartment. I had never searched his things before, but I needed answers.

The first thing I saw was a stack of folded papers. I opened them up and read the title on the front page: 'Child Support Hearing Requested.' My eyes widened as I scanned the page for the name of the custodial parent.

Finally, landing on Jessica Pearson, I breathed a sigh of relief. She was his daughter's mother. I already knew she had taken him to court since their daughter moved in with her full-time.

Flipping to the second page, I froze. This section asked for the names of his dependents, and I couldn't believe my eyes: Derek, Tyrone, Keisha, Keon, Keith, King, Kevin, and Katie.

"What?" I uttered faintly. Counting the names again, there were eight in total. "Eight kids! There's no way he has eight kids." At the start of our relationship, he only had one.

I looked at Katie and Kevin asleep in the back seat, and rage surged through me. I left them in the car and stormed into my apartment.

"You lied to me!" I shouted, with the fury of a woman who had just discovered she'd been betrayed.

"What the hell are you talking about now?" David sat up in the bed. "And where are the kids?"

"I left them in the car."

"In the car? Are you crazy?" He got up and went out the door, as I followed behind him.

"I found the child support papers. Why do you have eight kids listed as your dependents?"

He stopped in his tracks. "You searched my car?"

"Yeah, I did. Is that all you have to say?"

He opened the door, taking Kevin and Katie out of the car. "Listen, I had to list as many dependents as possible to keep my monthly payments low. They never ask for proof. They only ask you to list your dependents, so I put down every child I know."

Unsure of what to believe, I just stood there in silence.

"Do you actually believe I have eight kids?" he shook his head. "I thought you were smarter than that, but I guess not."

"I'm sorry. You've been acting so strange lately that I don't know what to believe anymore," I said, feeling foolish.

"I already explained why I haven't been around as much. If you can't understand, that's on you. But one thing's for sure, this is the first and last time you'll ever drive my car," he said, walking off and taking the kids into the house.

I followed behind him, frantically thinking of a way to smooth things over. "I'm sorry," I pleaded.

"Yeah, yeah, you're always sorry." He walked past me and slammed the front door.

After I put the kids down for a nap, I called David repeatedly to apologize, but he didn't answer. I was so upset with myself. "How foolish of me to search his things?"

As I paced the floor, there was a knock at the door. I knew it wasn't him because he had a key, and none of my friends or family came to visit because of the distance, so it could only be someone from the leasing office.

My rent was late again, and I was avoiding them until I had the money.

I tiptoed to the door and looked out the peephole; it was a lady and a little girl. "Who is it?" I asked.

"It's Mrs. Green from Florida National College. We spoke on the phone the other day," she announced.

I was confused. I had called the school to inquire about their accounting program, but I didn't expect anyone to make a house call.

I opened the door and stuck my head out.

"Hi, Sabrena?" She greeted me with a smile.

"Yes, how can I help you?"

"We talked on the phone the other day; I was in the neighborhood and figured I'd stop by."

Are you kidding me? was my initial thought. "I'm sorry, but this is not a good time."

"I don't mean to interrupt your day; I just want to encourage you to really consider going back to school."

"I'm not sure," I confessed, suddenly realizing how insane it was to entertain the idea of college, having no job and three little ones to care for.

"Why not? You want to give your children the best life possible, don't you?"

"Of course I do," I said, fighting back tears. It seemed like all I did most days was cry.

"Well, darling, I'm here to tell you that nobody can change the course of your life, but you. You have to do it for yourself," she said, sternly.

Before departing, she gave me the enrollment forms and information about their accounting program. I placed them on the counter, too consumed with worry about reconciling with David to consider anything else.

As night fell, I settled down to watch television when the phone rang. Relieved that David had finally returned my call, I answered without checking the caller ID.

"Hey," I said, prepared to deliver the apology speech I'd rehearsed all afternoon.

"Hello, who is this?" said the voice on the other end.

"This is Sabrena. Who is this?"

There was silence on the line, so I repeated the question. "Who's calling?"

"I was washing my husband's clothes and found your number."

"Well, I just got this number. Maybe it was the person who had it before me," I said, disappointed it wasn't the call I had been expecting.

There was another pause, and then she spoke, "But the paper has your name on it."

That's odd. The only person I had given my new number to was Da… "What's your husband's name?"

"His name is David, David Hall."

"David?! What do you mean David is your husband?"

"Yes, that's correct," she asserted, "It's a common law marriage. We've been together for ten years, but we plan on making it official soon."

"Is this some sort of joke? David has been my boyfriend for six years, and he is the father of my kids," I said, convinced someone was pranking me.

"The father of your kids? How many kids do you have?"

"I have three, but two of them are twins."

"What?! I have twins with him, too," she announced.

Like a brick to the face, those words knocked me out of my denial and into the harsh reality of the moment. A million thoughts raced through my mind, but I focused on just one. "Is this Linda?"

"Yes, that's correct. David and I live together."

"So, you're not his God-sister?" I was dumbfounded.

"God-sister? No, honey, I'm his wife."

In a heartbeat, my world shattered, along with the remnants of my self-esteem. "That explains why he doesn't sleep over anymore, or why he's never in the mood for sex. He said he's been too stressed to even think about it." I spoke more to myself than to her. Nonetheless, she had a response.

"Too stressed for sex? Sweetheart, we're intimate just about every night."

She was clearly determined to establish herself as his primary woman, and me, as the side chick. The message was becoming abundantly clear when suddenly, she broke down.

"I can't believe he cheated on me again," she cried. "I knew about Ebony, but not you. So that means he now has," she paused, "eight kids!"

I couldn't think. I couldn't speak. All I could do was end the call, so I did.

Chapter 11

From Darkness to Light

'Ten years! That means he's been deceiving me since the day we met.' I recalled all the names listed on the child support paper, and my body went numb.

How could he have eight kids? I just couldn't wrap my mind around it. "Ebony, why does that name sound familiar?" Then it struck me; Ebony was the girl who came to his house back when we first started dating. I was nauseated.

"I'm so stupid!" I screamed, throwing my phone.

"I had three kids by the age of twenty-two, and he's been cheating since day one?"

I couldn't move.

I recalled the night I had to beg him for intimacy. He stopped by to drop off a box of diapers, and I was so lonely for attention that I literally begged for it. 'Yet, according to Linda, they had sex every night!'

Staring at the red streaks on the living room wall, my eyes traced the lines to the bottle of Nyquil on the kitchen counter. "My life is ruined, and it's all been a lie?"

I got up.

"No man is ever going to want a single mother with three kids."

I walked to the counter.

"I don't have a car, a job or anything else except a bunch of babies, and he's in a common law marriage with his 'God-sister' Linda?"

Before I realized it, I was standing in the kitchen holding the bottle of Nyquil in my hand.

"Nobody calls, nobody visits, and nobody cares."

Blinded by my tears, I removed the cap and glared at the red liquid inside. Then, I closed my eyes and downed the bottle.

I fixed my eyes on the school enrollment forms. The girl on the front cover seemed so happy. Dressed in a navy-blue business suit, she held the suitcase with confidence. As I stared at her, I couldn't help but think... that was supposed to be me.

As time went on, a wave of dizziness came over me, and my hands and lips began to tremble. I went to the bedroom and crawled into bed with Kevin, who was sound asleep. Looking over at Katie and King, and then back at Kevin—still the most adorable little human I'd ever seen—I cried uncontrollably.

As drowsiness overtook me, I gazed at the crib once more. 'No, I can't leave them here like this. I just can't.'

I picked up the phone and dialed 911.

THE LIFTER OF MY HEAD

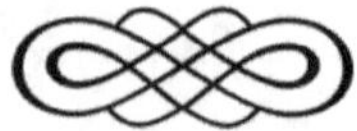

I was walking around with my head hung low

Desperately seeking which way to go

Heartache and disappointment at every turn

Major life lessons are the hardest to learn

I cried and I tried to figure it out

Just what this thing called life was about

Then a small voice from deep within said

Just look towards Jesus, the lifter of your head.

From Darkness to Light

After explaining my actions to the 911 operator, both the fire rescue and police were dispatched. They promptly administered smelling salts to keep me alert and provided me with charcoal to drink. "The Nyquil is slowly poisoning your system," explained the medic. "I need you to drink this fast, or I'll have to run a tube in your nose."

The police contacted my dad to pick up the kids since David was unreachable.

Under the Baker Act, I was handcuffed, placed in the ambulance, and transported to the hospital. Upon arrival, I was given another cup of thick black liquid, and my blood was tested for toxins.

"Now tell me, why would such a pretty young lady want to do something like this?" asked the police officer who accompanied me to the hospital.

I looked at him and began to weep all over again.

"Hey, I didn't mean to make you cry. Okay, let's change the subject."

"What's going to happen to me now?" I asked, growing concerned.

"Well, because you were trying to harm yourself, under the Baker Act, you have to be committed for at least 24 hours."

"Committed? Like a psychiatric patient?"

He looked away, and a wave of depression washed over me. "The psychiatric hospital is just across the street. Once we're finished here, I'll need to take you over there," he sincerely stated.

"I'm not crazy. I just need a break from all of this," I said, trying to convince myself.

"I understand, and I'm sure you'll receive the help you need over there."

At that moment, the hospital social worker approached us. "Hi Sabrena, I heard you drank a bottle of Nyquil," she spoke slowly, as if addressing a mental patient.

Ashamed, I nodded slightly.

"Why did you do that, sweetie? Did you want to kill yourself?" Hearing those words out loud helped me realize that was the last thing I wanted to do.

"Do you mind not talking so loudly?" the officer interjected. "We are in the hallway."

Glancing around, I caught the eyes of a few observers, including nurses. I looked down at my arm handcuffed to the gurney and shook my head.

"So, why did you do it then?" she pressed further.

Grief welled up, choking my throat. All I could muster was a faint, "I don't know."

Once more, the officer intervened, "I think that's enough for right now. She has to finish drinking this before the doctor comes back."

"Can I have a word with you in private, officer?" asked the social worker.

He turned to me and smiled, "I want that cup empty by the time I get back, okay?"

As I watched him walk away, I wondered if he genuinely thought I was pretty. I was so desperate for attention that I couldn't recognize when someone was simply being kind.

After I had completely digested the charcoal, the doctor ordered more tests to ensure there wasn't any underlying damage. Luckily, the bottle of Nyquil wasn't full, so all the tests came back normal.

Once discharged, I was transported across the street in the back of a police car. That moment surpassed the day at the abortion clinic as the lowest point of my life.

Upon entering the building, the doors locked behind us. He handed a paper to the receptionist and guided me to the waiting room.

"This is our final stop, Ms. Sabrena. I wish you the very best." He gave me a slight hug and walked out the double doors into the summer night.

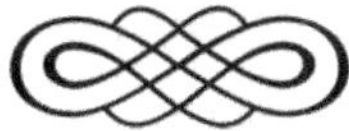

The entire night felt surreal. I sat in the waiting room, feeling lifeless. I just stared at the floor, and pondered about the road ahead. Would I lose my children? Would I be classified as mentally ill? How could my life go so horribly wrong in such a short period of time?

My thoughts shifted to David Hall, the man who went to great lengths to deceive me and turn my world upside down... or did he?

Did he truly go to great lengths when the writing was on the wall all along? How could I not have asked to meet Linda? She's driven his car for years, even while I rode the bus.

I thought back on the night he took me out to dinner when I was pregnant with Kevin.

He saw another pregnant woman standing outside the window, told me he'd be right back, and returned twenty minutes later with the only explanation being that she was a friend of the family who needed to talk.

Reflecting on that incident, along with numerous others, I had to wonder: was it David's Deception or my own? Did I deceive myself into believing that the simple notion of having a man was enough to cover up the emptiness I held inside?

Truth be told, I was broken when we met, and it showed. The question becomes: where did it originate from, and why did I believe a relationship could fix it?

I was deep in thought when the lobby door opened. Like a knight in shining armor, my step-dad James appeared. I was so relieved to see a familiar face that I sprang to my feet and rushed over to him. "Sabrena, are you okay?" he asked, his eyes full of concern.

"Yes," I nodded.

"You know you could've come to us if you needed help. We will always be here for you," he said, giving me a warm hug.

His words provided more comfort than he would ever know.

"Come on, we're leaving," he added.

I glanced at the receptionist and then back at him. "Are we going to sneak out?" I whispered, not entirely opposed to the idea.

"They're letting you go home. You don't want to be in a place like this."

'Truer words had never been spoken,' I thought to myself.

James was a long-time fire lieutenant who had many connections in the city. After learning that I was going to be Baker Acted, he called in a few favors and had me released.

And just like that, off we went to confront the harsh realities of my present situation.

My Moment of Realization

The following morning, my dad brought the kids to my mom's house, and we stayed there for a couple of days. Family and friends stopped by to see me, offering uplifting words of encouragement.

I shared everything about David and my phone conversation with Linda. "You're better off without him," my mom said, shaking her head. "Didn't a company in Fort Lauderdale offer you a job recently?"

"Yes, but I don't have a way to get there," I said.

"James and I have decided to lend you the money to get a car. Nothing too expensive, and you can take your time to pay it back."

"Thank you, Jesus!" Those words were like music to my ears. No more hauling that stroller onto the bus or enduring that walk of shame to the bus stop.

At the end of the week, we returned home. With my spirits lifted, I felt prepared to confront the mystery man whose identity had finally been revealed. Once I reached home, I called him, and he came right over.

"Are you okay?" David asked. "I tried calling you after I heard what happened, but your phone kept going to voicemail."

"I'm better now," I stated. "We have to meet with a social worker from the Department of Children and Families on Monday."

"What do you mean, 'we'? What do I have to do with this?"

Seriously? "They are your kids too, David. They want to make sure this is a safe environment for them."

He sucked his teeth. "What were you thinking anyway? I'm sure you feel silly now that everyone is treating you like you're suicidal."

The stark contrast between the love and support I received from others, and the negativity radiating from him was glaring. "You know what? For the past three days, all I have received were words of encouragement. So, if you don't have anything positive to say, please leave!"

"What do you want me to say? I'm sorry you tried to kill yourself? Do you know how that sounds?"

I peered at him through eyes that had finally regained their sight, and what I saw was nothing worth holding onto, let alone dying for. "David, from this point forward, you don't have to say anything to me at all."

I walked to the door. "If you don't mind, I have to give my attention back to my kids."

"Are you going to be alright in here with them?" he asked, in a calmer tone.

"We are going to be just fine," I said with confidence.

He lingered for a moment, contemplating whether he should leave or stay. He walked over to Katie and gave her a kiss, then rubbed King and Kevin on the head before walking towards the door. Stopping, he turned to face me.

"Hey, I'm sorry you had to find out about everything this way. Linda never should've called you."

That was the final straw. The unconditional love that consumed me for years suddenly had all kinds of conditions, one of which being, he could no longer play me for a fool.

"You're right! I shouldn't have had to discover that the man I love, the only man I've ever been with, has been lying and cheating since the day we met. The same man I fought battles with my parents over. The same man I ran away from home to be with. The same man who robbed me of my hopes and dreams and left me here alone to struggle with three babies at the age of twenty-two.

You're absolutely correct; I shouldn't have had to find out from his common-law wife, a.k.a. God-sister Linda, that he is a cheating, manipulative, compulsive liar. I should've heard it from YOU!"

He stood there in silence, which only fueled my anger. "Get out of my house, David!" I demanded.

He lingered a while longer and then finally said, "I'll check on you guys later," as he walked out the door.

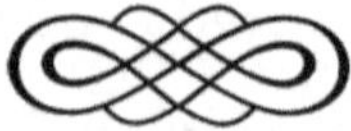

With boldness in my heart, I refused to shed another tear for a man who couldn't muster up an ounce of remorse for me. I walked to the counter and picked up the school enrollment forms. Staring at the girl on the front page, I declared with unwavering faith: "This will be me."

"Mommy, look," Kevin exclaimed.

I turned just in time to see King take his first steps across the living room floor. "Oh, my goodness! You're finally walking, baby!" I scooped him up and kissed his little cheek. "I knew you could do it."

I watched Katie attempt to push Kevin on his bike and laughed, 'Humph, you know what? I actually like kids.'

Observing my babies, for the first time I saw them as the blessings they truly were. I held King in my arms and smiled at my moment of realization. It was the moment I grasped the true meaning of love. It wasn't found in a man; it was embraced in the eyes of my children and through the comforting peace of knowing that Jesus was right there with me. I also realized there were far worse things than being alone—like being broken, unhappy, with low self-esteem, and not allowing yourself the time and space to discover the root cause and to heal.

At that moment, I made a commitment to take the broken pieces of the puzzle that made up my life and, with the help of God, create an image that I could be proud of... and that's exactly what I did.

My New Journey

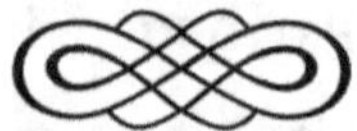

Twisted roads with shattered glass
Broken pieces of innocence lost
Lies, lies and alibis

We all have roads to travel in this life
It's what shapes us into who we are
My life has taken me down many roads

Roads of pain, shame and gain

Pain from the loss of my first love
Heartache over the depth of his lies
Shame over the aftermath...three kids at twenty-two

Yes, I lost a love that wasn't real love
But what I gained was so much more
Three beautiful reasons for living
Three hearts of my very own

That beats for me, with me, and through me

Now my roads have changed
No more heartache over past hurt and pain
I've taken off my mask of shame

New roads shape my future
Roads of pride, determination and love

Pride that drives me
Determination that guides me
And love to make it all
worthwhile

EPILOGUE

I wish I could say that my relationship with David concluded that day with the closing of my front door, a symbolic end to our story. I would like to declare that as the final chapter, but I can't.

In truth, I endured a few more years of the same toxic behavior.

And after he and Linda officially tied the knot, I transitioned from unknowingly being the woman on the side to willingly being his mistress. It wasn't until his wife mistreated my children, and he allowed it, that I finally walked away.

So, why did I endure it? Why did I cling to a man who obviously didn't care about me or my feelings?

The answer is deeply rooted in several factors, the greatest of all being fear.

I feared the idea of being alone so much that I failed to realize I was already alone—all those nights I stayed awake waiting for him and he never showed up, and all those days I had to take care of our children by myself— I was alone. At a certain point, I was in a relationship with the thought of the man, rather than the man himself. But at the time, I didn't see it.

All I knew was that I needed our relationship to mask an insecurity I held about myself long before I met him, and because I didn't take the time to do the work internally, I continued to make desperate decisions externally.

This pattern repeated itself for years in subsequent relationships, even after I went back to school, obtained multiple degrees and secured a corporate job.

Why? Because the greatest deception of the enemy is convincing us that intertwining ourselves with another person is enough to fill our voids.

In truth, when a broken woman connects with a broken man, the only outcome is more brokenness — because healing is an inside job. It takes more than mere words to bring about change; it requires time alone with God and a significant amount of time spent getting to know yourself. —The Real You.

In hindsight, I understand that the root of my issue was a fear of rejection, originating from childhood experiences. This fear drove me to relentlessly seek David's acceptance, even when it became evident that it wasn't worth obtaining.

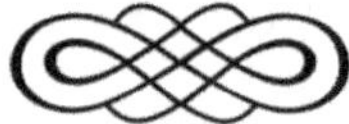

Oftentimes, we are indeed blinded in the areas where we need healing the most. We seek God for answers, hoping that the ones He provides support our agenda.

I was convinced the solution to my problem was to 'rekindle the flames with David.' However, God intervened and completely turned my situation around, revealing a truth that seemed too painful to bear. While it wasn't the answer I desired, it was certainly the one I needed.

With the help of my parents, I bought a car, accepted the pending job offer, and indeed enrolled in college— as a single parent of three small children.

Today, I hold a master's degree, run my own business, am a certified life purpose coach, have a loving husband, and live a happy and peaceful life.

That's why suicide is never the answer. The day I believed my life was ending, actually marked the start of a bold new beginning.

Never surrender the promises of tomorrow to the temporary circumstances of today, for there's truly no dead place in your life that God doesn't have the power to resurrect—according to His perfect will.

In conclusion, I felt compelled to share my story because I encounter women who grapple with their own personal 'David' every day: the wife who turns a blind eye as her husband spends time with his mistress, the middle-aged woman who allows her partner to belittle her and make her feel inadequate, and the girlfriend who sees the red flags, but disregards them, out of fear and low self-esteem.

Oh, but there's a better way —God's way. The love of Jesus is far from deceitful; it's genuine, pure, and compassionate. It possesses the power to heal years of hurt, pain, and insecurities, establishing a set of standards that not even the most cunning 'Davids' can eradicate. It is my earnest prayer that everyone comes to experience His love in this profound way.

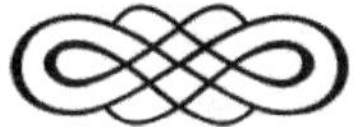

Always Remember:

God Sees You, and He Cares!

ABOUT THE AUTHOR

Consultant, Speaker, and Coach Sabrena Jay-Songowa is a transformative force in the realm of personal and spiritual development. Since founding Sabrena Jay Inspirations in 2016, she has dedicated herself to guiding individuals toward freedom from defeated mindsets, past hurts, and negative self-truths.

As a life purpose coach, she leads clients through 8 transformative weeks of Purpose Coaching sessions, clearing the path for God's true purpose to shine.

Sabrena has appeared on television, Christian talk radio, podcasts, hosted purpose coaching workshops, delivered corporate lectures, and inspired audiences with her most requested talk on How to Discover Your Purpose and Pursue It.

Sjiconsulting.net

Sjinspirations.com

Enjoyed Reading David's Deception? Please leave a review on the platform of your purchase to help others decide!